MORE FIRED UP

NO NONSENSE BARBECUING

MORE
NO NONSENSE
BARBECUING
FIRED UP

ROSS DOBSON

MURDOCH BOOKS

CONTENTS

METAL ON HEAT.
MEAT ON METAL .

SINCE I WROTE THE ORIGINAL *FIRED UP*, LITTLE HAS CHANGED in the world of barbecuing. Actually, one might say little has changed in the world of barbecuing since the dawn of man, give or take a few minor advancements, such as the Iron Age and discovery of fossil fuels. But, really, it is all pretty much the same. It's back to basics—using heat to cook food by the most elemental means available. Fire.

Barbecuing, well my notion of barbecuing, is about producing tasty, no nonsense food. This is my mantra. When I worked on the recipes for *Fired Up* I had little more than the most basic of barbecues. A grill plate and a hotplate set over some gas burners with a rather flimsy lid. All the same, I was pretty bloody happy with what my old barbecue produced—simple, tasty, no nonsense food.

I had that barbecue for six happy years. It was hard to let go when its time was up. It wasn't until rust won out and the burners simply disintegrated that I was forced to say goodbye. But there were exciting times ahead as I went in search of a new barbecue. A sturdy, sexy, stainless steel number, with a lid, a window to perve through and a thermometer.

I use my new barbecue as an oven of sorts. Most of the modern barbecues have lids and mine, with its stainless steel casing, both conducts and radiates heat really well. So, when cooking big cuts of meat, like whole lamb and pork shoulders, rib eye roast, sides of sirloin, even whole chickens and fish, I preheat the grill and hotplate burners to high and close the lid. You will see the thermometer rise and the internal temperature will act like that in an oven. So when you put the pork or whatever in, the skin will immediately start to cook. You can of course then turn the temperature down and cook the meat to your liking.

In barbecuing I can never deny my roots. I am Australian with a unique attitude towards barbecuing. I relish in our cultural diversity, which brings to us food, flavours and influences from afar. Combine our style of cooking and access to such fine ingredients and you have really tasty food that can be made with ease. And fancy barbecue or not, I think this is how most of us like to barbecue. A few flavours and a flame later, you have something that you can't wait to cook again.

In a sense, barbecuing allows us to be masters, or mistresses, of our domain.

We are the masters of flavour. It really is up to you how the food will taste. It really is up to you how tender the meat is, in terms of cooking time and utilising different cuts of meat. Before the meat goes on the barbecue, remember to season well just before cooking and once on, don't continuously (and mindlessly!) turn the meat on the barbecue and always allow the meat to rest after being cooked.

I am lucky enough to have a front verandah with room to spare for my barbecue and me. It is one of those federation-style verandahs with no logical explanation as to why exactly it needs to be so big. But who's complaining? It's a beauty. Sun-drenched and north-facing, with just the right amount of shade. Rain, hail or shine, summer or winter, I can barbecue to my heart's content on the front verandah, waving at neighbours and passers-by. Sound sociable? It is. Barbecuing is as much about having fun as anything else. Relax, enjoy, and you are halfway there to really good food.

A FEW SIMPLE HOT TIPS

YOUR FOOD

Preheat the barbecue before cooking. You want to hear a healthy sizzle as the food hits the hotplate or grill. A barbecue is not for stewing or simmering.

Closing the lid of the barbecue will keep the heat in and create a hot-oven effect. Even if I'm only using part of the barbecue, I sometimes turn all the burners on and close the lid. So when the food is put on the barbecue (like a leg of lamb, a turkey breast or beef fillet) it will start to cook immediately and the internal heat will cook it evenly and quickly.

Before you even think of cooking the food, remove it from the fridge. This is really important. A fridge-cold, thick steak cooked to rare will still be cold in the centre. Chicken is another story of course. It does have nasty bugs, which can make people sick, but not all meat has the same bugs. It doesn't work that way. Let your beef, lamb and pork come to room temperature before cooking. Food hygiene is important but let's not get too carried away.

Season your food well before cooking but not too far in advance or it will make the meat tough. A light sprinkling of sea salt 30 minutes prior to cooking is all that's needed.

Always allow meat to rest after cooking. Give big bits of meat, like whole sirloin, beef fillet or whole birds, a good 20–30 minutes rest, covered with some cooking foil. Steaks will need less time to rest, but do rest them nonetheless.

A hot surface will actually prevent the food from sticking. And allowing the food to develop a crust lets you turn the food without it tearing. This is especially the case with fish skin. (And keep in mind that defrosted, frozen fish is a nightmare to turn without tearing or breaking the flesh. Cooking the fish on a sheet of baking paper will prevent this.)

And for some reason when we are standing at the barbecue we do feel like we need to incessantly do stuff to the food, like constantly turning the meat. Don't do this as it will ruin the meat. Except for sausages. They don't count and you can turn them as often as you like.

YOUR EQUIPMENT

Keep your barbecue reasonably clean but don't go overboard. I know a guy who actually uses an angle grinder to clean his hotplate. This is a tad extreme—but he does do the best crispy-skinned fish on it!

Some people recommend cleaning the barbecue while it is hot. But who wants to do that? When you finish cooking you really just want to be with the people you have cooked for, not putting the cleaning gloves on. To clean, simply use a bit of warm soapy water and some elbow grease. Turn the barbecue on low heat to dry it out then wipe over with some cooking oil—this will help prevent rust from setting in.

If you really want to clean the barbie while it is still hot, I reckon the best thing to do is give it a good hosing down. This will get rid of most of the gunk and the water will evaporate super fast, reducing rust. (In taking this option, I am assuming your barbecue is in a backyard and not on an apartment balcony.)

Speaking of rust, this is something out of our control, considering most barbecues are left outdoors, year round. If the hotplates or grills start to rust it is time to replace them, people. And do look at the burners underneath. Rusty burners can collapse mid-barbie. (That would be a disaster, and somewhat disconcerting.) Replacing these things is neither expensive nor difficult. New hotplates and grills are sold separately at barbecue stores. I actually use a barbecue hotplate on the gas hobs on my kitchen stove for some pretty good indoor grilling results.

SOMETHING HAPPENED SOME TIME AGO WHEN WE MOVED away from a diet dominated by meat and two veg to chicken. Roasted, poached, stir-fried, souped up, fried and, of course, barbecued. I do wonder whether our love of the chook has something to do with a greater awareness of healthy eating. But healthy eating is something that does not always influence what I eat. I go for flavour. And sad though it may be, fat equals flavour. It's the tiny bits of fat on the thigh and drumstick that make this cut taste so good. I am not really a breast man unless it has the skin on, which keeps the meat protected from the intense heat of the barbecue (not to mention the fact the crispy chicken skin actually adds flavour).

Chook (or, for those non-Antipodeans out there, chicken) is a bit of a tart, really, as it goes with many flavours. Use lots of fresh chilli, garlic and ginger. For herbs go coriander, parsley, oregano and thyme. Bathe your chicken in soy sauce, wine or citrus prior to cooking for extra flavour. World over, the chook may well be the creature most eaten.

The bird serves us well. Thighs, breasts, wings, drumsticks. On the bone or off. Skin on or off. Filleted or cubed and skewered. And if that weren't enough, we also love the other bits like the liver.

The coop does take some poetic licence. It also houses other feathered creatures; quail and duck in particular—both very tasty birds.

But nothing is quite as tasty as the chook. One bird made to barbecue.

SPECIAL BRINED ROAST CHICKEN WITH AÏOLI

Serves 4

Brining is not something you want to do every day, or every time you barbecue, but the resulting flavour of a brined chicken (or turkey for that matter) is very special indeed. Brining is pure science. It's osmosis. It's about getting flavour from one place to another. It does require some planning but is well worth the effort.

INGREDIENTS
520 g (1 lb 2 oz/2 cups) cooking salt
250 ml (9 fl oz/1 cup) white wine
    vinegar
1 tablespoon fennel seeds
2 bay leaves
2 small chickens, about 1.2 kg
    (2 lb 10 oz) each

AÏOLI
2 egg yolks
2 garlic cloves, crushed
pinch white pepper
1 tablespoon lemon juice
185 ml (6 fl oz/¾ cup) rice bran oil

METHOD
Put the salt, vinegar, fennel seeds and bay leaves in a large saucepan with 10–12 litres (340–405 fl oz/42–51 cups) of cold water. Bring to the boil, then reduce the heat and simmer for 30 minutes. Remove from the heat and allow to cool to room temperature.

Cut the chickens in half lengthways between the breasts, immerse them in the brining solution and refrigerate for 6 hours or overnight. Remove the chicken, discard the solution and place the chicken, skin side up, on a baking tray or a few large plates. Refrigerate for another 3–6 hours, removing them from the fridge 30 minutes before cooking.

To make the aïoli, put the egg yolks, garlic, white pepper and lemon juice in the bowl of a small food processor and whiz to combine. With the motor running very slowly, add the rice bran oil in a steady stream. Continue adding the oil until you have a creamy custard or mayonnaise-like consistency. Transfer to a bowl.

Preheat the barbecue hotplate and grill to high and close the lid to create a hot-oven effect. Sit the chicken skin side up on a rack and sit the rack over a deep baking tray. Half fill the baking tray with water and place it on the barbecue. Close the lid and cook for 40–45 minutes, until the skin is golden. Remove from the barbecue and allow to rest for 10–15 minutes.

Serve the chicken with the aïoli on the side, and chargrilled baby carrots, if desired.

CHICKEN WITH JALAPEÑO BUTTER

Serves 4

A couple of my fave things here—jalapeños in brine and chicken breast with skin. There seemed a time when we all obsessed about skinless chicken breasts. And what an odd obsession, don't you think? Leaving the skin on makes all the difference when it comes to flavour. Even if you don't like the skin (you can always put it aside—someone else at the table is bound to snap it up) leaving it on during cooking will make the breast lovely and tender. As for jalapeños, I use them all the time in salsas with corn, in mayonnaise and even Chinese stir-fries with pork or duck.

METHOD

To make the jalapeño butter, put all the ingredients in a food processor and whiz until well combined. Transfer to a bowl.

Rub as much of the butter mixture as you can under the skin of the chicken breasts, being careful not to break the skin. Rub any remaining butter over the skin and sprinkle with a little sea salt. You can secure the skin with toothpicks. This will help prevent the skin from retracting when cooked.

Preheat the barbecue hotplate to high and close the lid to create a hot-oven effect. Sit the chicken on a rack and sit the rack over a deep baking tray. Half fill the baking tray with water and sit it on the barbecue. Close the lid and cook for 35–40 minutes, until the skin is golden. Remove from the barbecue and allow to rest for 10–15 minutes.

Serve with the lime halves and coriander.

JALAPEÑO BUTTER

2 tablespoons sliced jalapeños
   in brine, drained
1 garlic clove, chopped
1 large handful coriander
   (cilantro) leaves
2 anchovy fillets in oil, drained
125 g (4½ oz) unsalted butter,
   softened to room temperature

4 chicken breasts, with wings
   attached and skin on
lime halves, to serve
fresh coriander (cilantro) leaves,
   to serve

CHICKEN WITH BACON AND WITLOF

Serves 6

Endive loses some of its bitter intensity when cooked, and this isn't a bad thing. You could throw the ingredients of this recipe between a lovely, soft burger bun with some aïoli. Or even sprinkle some grated parmesan cheese over the top— a bit like a chicken Caesar salad.

INGREDIENTS

6 large boneless, skinless
    chicken thighs
12 streaky bacon slices
3 tablespoons olive oil
1 tablespoon red wine vinegar
1 garlic clove, finely chopped
2 tablespoons roughly chopped
    flat-leaf (Italian) parsley, plus
    extra sprigs, to serve
ground white pepper
4 endive or large witlof
    (chicory/Belgian endive),
    quartered
lemon cheeks, to serve

METHOD

Cut each chicken thigh in half. Wrap a slice of bacon around the middle of each thigh and sit in a flat dish.

Mix together the olive oil, vinegar, garlic and parsley in a bowl, pour over the chicken and toss to coat. Set aside at room temperature for 30 minutes, or cover and refrigerate for 3–6 hours.

Remove the chicken from the fridge 30 minutes before cooking.

Season the chicken well with sea salt and ground white pepper. Preheat the barbecue grill and hotplate to high.

Cut the witlof in half lengthways. Put the cut side of the witlof down on the grill. Put the chicken on the hotplate and close the lid. Cook for 8–10 minutes, so the witlof is well browned and the bacon and chicken golden. Turn both witlof and chicken over, close the lid and cook for another 5 minutes.

Arrange the witlof and chicken randomly on a serving platter and scatter over the extra parsley. Serve with the lemon cheeks on the side.

TANDOORI CHICKEN

Serves 4

I cannot claim to have invented the technique of sitting the chicken on a beer can. However, I just love the idea and the results. It is also the most ideal way to barbecue a whole bird, when many of us do not have a rotisserie built in to our barbecue. And this chicken is so good on grilled Indian naan bread, with some shredded lettuce and lemon squeezed over.

INGREDIENTS

1 teaspoon saffron threads
2 small chickens, about 1.2 kg
    (2 lb 10 oz) each
125 ml (4 fl oz/½ cup) lemon juice
3 teaspoons sea salt
2 onions, chopped
260 g (9¼ oz/1 cup) plain yoghurt
2 tablespoons ghee
2 garlic cloves, chopped
1 tablespoon finely grated ginger
2 teaspoons ground cumin
1 teaspoon ground coriander
½ teaspoon ground turmeric
½ teaspoon chilli powder

METHOD

Soak the saffron threads in 2 tablespoons of hot water for 10 minutes.

Wash the chickens and pat dry with paper towel. Cut two deep slashes into the breasts and legs of each bird and put into a large bowl. Combine the lemon juice, sea salt and saffron mixture in a small bowl and pour over the chicken. Toss to coat and rub the mixture into the slashes. Set aside at room temperature for 30 minutes.

Put the onion, yoghurt, ghee, garlic, ginger, cumin, coriander, turmeric and chilli powder in a food processor and blend to a paste. Rub all over the chicken. Cover and refrigerate for 6 hours or overnight, turning the chicken every now and then.

Remove the chicken from the fridge 30 minutes before cooking.

Preheat the barbecue burners to high and close the lid to create a hot-oven effect. Sit the cavity of each chicken on an empty beer can.

Reduce the heat to medium and sit the chicken upright on the hotplate so the can and the ends of the chicken drumsticks form a tripod. Close the lid and cook for 1 hour 10 minutes, or until golden and cooked through. The juices should run clear when the thigh is pierced with a skewer. Serve half a chicken per person.

FIERY THIGHS

Serves 4

A tip here for flavour success—use dried Greek oregano. You will find this at delis, hung in dry bushes in a plastic bag. It is much more flavoursome than most supermarket varieties and I reckon it even smells very different. Although I don't use many dried herbs, and there are some I will never use, this one I use more like a spice and I would even go so far as to say it is better than fresh oregano.

METHOD

As one end of the thigh is thicker than the other, pound the thicker end with a meat mallet so it is all the same thickness. Cut each thigh in half and put into a bowl with the oregano, chilli, sea salt, parsley, lemon juice and olive oil. Toss the chicken to coat in the marinade. Cover and set aside at room temperature for 30 minutes, or refrigerate for up to 6 hours or even overnight. Turn the chicken often if it is in the fridge and remove from the fridge 30 minutes before cooking.

Preheat the barbecue hotplate to high. Put the chicken on the hotplate, leaving the excess marinade in the bowl. Cook for 7–8 minutes. Pour over about half of the reserved marinade then turn the chicken over and cook for 5–6 minutes. Pour the remaining marinade over the chicken. Turn the chicken over on the hotplate a few times until the marinade is cooked off. Season with extra sea salt and serve with the lemon wedges.

INGREDIENTS

6 boneless, skinless chicken thighs
1 teaspoon dried Greek oregano
1 teaspoon chilli flakes
1 teaspoon sea salt, plus extra, to serve
2 tablespoons finely chopped flat-leaf (Italian) parsley
3 tablespoons lemon juice
3 tablespoons olive oil
lemon wedges, to serve

FRAGRANT CHICKEN PARCELS

Serves 4

Where would we be without Chinese food? Here we have some classic Chinese flavours—sweet and salty with intense aromatics. Tenderloins are great. They often don't need any cutting or chopping. I like their shape and size and use them all the time in curries, not even browned off, just thrown into the hot curry and left to poach. Here, the tenderloins are wrapped and steamed on the hotplate.

METHOD

Put all the ingredients in a bowl, tossing to combine. Set aside at room temperature for 30 minutes, or cover and refrigerate for up to 6 hours. Remove from the fridge 30 minutes before cooking.

Tear off four large sheets of foil and lay on a work surface. Tear off four large sheets of baking paper and lay each one on top of the foil.

Put 3 tenderloins in the centre of each sheet of baking paper. Use the foil to form a cup shape around the chicken. Spoon equal amounts of the marinade over each cup of chicken. Twist the foil to secure and enclose to make a parcel.

Preheat the barbecue hotplate to medium. Sit the parcels on the hotplate, close the lid and cook for 5–6 minutes or until cooked through.

Put the parcels on a platter to unwrap at the table. Garnish with fresh coriander leaves and serve with barbecued corn, if desired.

INGREDIENTS

12 chicken tenderloins
8 garlic cloves, peeled
3 tablespoons light soy sauce
50 g (1¾ oz) unsalted butter, melted
2 tablespoons honey
4 star anise
2 cinnamon sticks, broken in half
fresh coriander (cilantro) leaves, to serve

CHICKEN THIGHS WITH GARLIC CREAM

Serves 6

Trim the fat off the chicken thighs if you must, but I would encourage you to leave it on. Most of it will render off and sizzle away and it acts as a buffer between the thigh meat and the intense heat of the barbecue, leaving the thigh tender and very tasty. But the real star here is the toum, or garlic sauce. This is the toothsome stuff you most definitely would find at any good Lebanese restaurant. Think of it as similar to but also very different from aïoli. It has no yolks just egg whites and tastes so bloody good.

GARLIC CREAM
4 garlic cloves, chopped
2 egg whites
185 ml (6 fl oz/¾ cup) olive oil

6 large boneless, skinless chicken
    thighs
125 ml (4 fl oz/½ cup) lemon juice
125 ml (4 fl oz/½ cup) white wine
2 teaspoons sea salt
1 teaspoon sugar
1 teaspoon dried oregano
flat-leaf (Italian) parsley leaves,
    to serve

METHOD
To make the garlic cream, put the garlic and egg whites into the bowl of a food processor and whiz to combine. With the motor running, slowly add the olive oil until the mixture is fluffy, white and creamy. Transfer to a bowl.

Combine the chicken, lemon juice, white wine, sea salt, sugar and oregano in a non-metallic dish. Set aside at room temperature for 30 minutes, or cover and refrigerate for 3–6 hours. Remove the chicken from the fridge 30 minutes before cooking.

Preheat the barbecue grill to high. Cook the thighs for 8 minutes. Turn over and cook for another 5 minutes.

Sprinkle with the parsley leaves and serve with the garlic cream.

CHILLI BEAN CHICKEN WRAPS

Serves 4

Chilli bean sauce is a combo of soy beans, chilli and vinegar. Many brands are available, some too intense even for my palate. Burritos and Chinese flavours might seem incongruous anywhere else except when barbecuing, which is all about using flavours, ingredients and techniques that work for you, right?

INGREDIENTS

3 tablespoons Chinese chilli
    bean sauce
1 teaspoon sesame oil
2 teaspoons light soy sauce
1 bunch coriander (cilantro),
    chopped
3 boneless, skinless chicken breasts
olive oil, for cooking
80 g (2¾ oz) shredded lettuce
1 Lebanese (short) cucumber,
    thinly sliced
4 soft burritos

METHOD

Put the chilli bean sauce, sesame oil, soy sauce and coriander in a food processor and process to a smooth paste. Tip into a bowl with the chicken, tossing the chicken to coat in the marinade. Cover and refrigerate for 3–6 hours or overnight, turning often.

Remove the chicken from the fridge 30 minutes before cooking. Preheat the barbecue grill to medium. Lightly brush the grill with olive oil to grease. Lay the chicken on the grill, close the lid and cook for 10 minutes. Turn over, close the lid and cook for another 8–10 minutes, or until cooked through. Remove and allow to rest for 10–15 minutes.

Thinly slice the chicken across the grain. Serve the sliced chicken, lettuce and cucumber on a burrito.

FESTIVE TURKEY WITH CRANBERRY AND CHERRY SAUCE

Serves 4

Marinating turkey breast is a good start to a tasty cooked bird. Leaving the skin on will also help prevent the meat from drying out. Cook the turkey until just done, wrap in foil and allow to rest.

METHOD

To make the cranberry and cherry sauce, combine the port, crème de cassis, chicken stock and cornflour in a small saucepan, stirring so the mixture is lump-free. Add the cherries, cranberries, cinnamon and sugar and simmer over medium heat for 4–5 minutes, until the liquid has thickened and the fruit is just tender. Set aside.

Preheat the barbecue hotplate and grill to high and cover with the lid to create a hot-oven effect. Reduce the heat to medium. Sprinkle sea salt over the skin of the turkey and lay the turkey, skin side down, on the hotplate. You will want to hear a gentle sizzle as the turkey hits the hotplate—if it is too hot, or sizzling too loudly, turn the heat down a little. Close the lid and cook for 15–20 minutes so the skin is golden and crisp. Turn over, close the lid and cook for another 10 minutes. Loosely wrap the turkey in foil and sit on the warm barbecue lid for 15 minutes, allowing the turkey to rest.

Carve the turkey, arrange on a serving plate and spoon over the cranberry and cherry sauce. Scatter over the sage leaves and serve.

CRANBERRY AND CHERRY SAUCE

170 ml (5½ fl oz/⅔ cup) port
4 tablespoons crème de cassis
2 tablespoons chicken stock
1 tablespoon cornflour (cornstarch)
125 g (4½ oz/¾ cup) fresh or frozen halved and pitted cherries
100 g (3½ oz/1 cup) fresh or frozen cranberries
½ teaspoon ground cinnamon
2 teaspoons sugar

1 boneless turkey breast, about 800 g (1 lb 12 oz), with skin on
1 handful sage leaves, to serve

MOROCCAN QUAIL WITH CUMQUAT

Serves 4

Moroccan cooking lends itself very well to the barbecue. Grilled meats, spiced with lots of ground cumin, coriander and paprika, are common in Morocco. And then there's the famous night food market in the Jamaa el Fna square in Marrakesh. The lights are pretty and romantic and the air thick with smoke from the coals of hundreds of grills. It has been proclaimed by the United Nations as a 'Masterpiece of the Oral and Intangible Heritage of Humanity'. Now that is some barbecue.

INGREDIENTS

8 quail
3 tablespoons orange juice
6 cumquats, halved
1 tablespoon tarragon vinegar
1 tablespoon olive oil
2 teaspoons ground coriander
coriander (cilantro) sprigs, to
    serve (optional)

METHOD

Sit a quail on a chopping board, breast side up. Insert a small sharp knife into the cavity of the quail and cut either side of the backbone. Remove and discard the backbone. Open the quail to flatten on the chopping board, so it is spatchcocked. With the palm of your hand, press down on the breastbone to flatten. Repeat with the remaining quail. Put the quail in a flat ceramic dish with the orange juice, cumquats, vinegar, olive oil and ground coriander. Toss the quail in the marinade and refrigerate, covered, for at least a couple of hours or up to 6 hours.

Remove the quail and cumquats from the marinade, put onto a tray and leave at room temperature for 30 minutes before cooking. Just before cooking, sprinkle sea salt over the quail.

Preheat the barbecue hotplate to medium. Cover the hotplate with a sheet of baking paper. Put the quail, skin side down, on the paper, close the lid and cook for 10 minutes, until they are aromatic and the skin crispy. Turn the quail over and strew the cumquats onto the hotplate. Cover and cook for another 4–5 minutes, until cooked through and the cumquats are softened and juicy.

Scatter with the coriander, if using, and serve with the cumquats and herbed couscous, if desired.

LEMON AND SPICE CHICKEN THIGHS

Serves 6

Again, I shall sing the praises of the chook thigh. And again I shall use spices common to Moroccan cooking. And if cooking is new to you or something that you find a challenge, then Moroccan recipes are the best place to start. Often dubbed Indian for beginners, Moroccan flavours and techniques are simple and uncomplicated. This is not to say they are not complex. And please remember, guys and gals, spices lose their potency. Buy them fresh and buy them often, preferably from specialty stores and, as they say, you will taste the difference.

METHOD

Combine the paprika, ginger, turmeric, coriander, olive oil and lemon juice in a small bowl. Put the chicken in a flat ceramic dish and pour over the marinade. Turn the chicken over a few times to coat in the marinade. Cover and refrigerate for a few hours or overnight, turning the chicken every now and then.

Remove the chicken from the fridge 30 minutes before cooking.

Preheat the barbecue hotplate to high. Put the thighs on the hotplate, sprinkle over some sea salt, and cook for 8 minutes, without moving them. Turn over and cook for another 4–5 minutes, until golden, aromatic and cooked through. Rest for a few minutes before serving.

INGREDIENTS

2 teaspoons paprika
2 teaspoons ground ginger
½ teaspoon ground turmeric
1 teaspoon ground coriander
3 tablespoons olive oil
2 tablespoons lemon juice
6 large boneless, skinless chicken thighs, each cut in half

BUCCANEER CHICKEN SKEWERS

Serves 4

Not too sure why I decided to title this one buccaneer, considering a buccaneer is someone who robs and plunders from the sea. I think it stems from an obsession with Caribbean food, which to me means lots of hot cayenne pepper and tropical lime—which brings buccaneers to mind!

INGREDIENTS

6 boneless, skinless chicken thighs,
    each cut into 4 pieces
2 spring onions (scallions), chopped
1 handful flat-leaf (Italian) parsley
2 garlic cloves, chopped
¼ teaspoon cayenne pepper
2 tablespoons lime juice
2 tablespoons olive oil

SAUCE

3 tablespoons lime juice
2 tablespoons olive oil
3 tablespoons finely chopped
    flat-leaf (Italian) parsley
2 teaspoons finely chopped
    rosemary
1 large red chilli, finely chopped
4 spring onions (scallions), thinly
    sliced

METHOD

Put the chicken in a ceramic dish or bowl. Put the spring onion, parsley, garlic, cayenne pepper, lime juice and olive oil in a food processor and process to a paste. Rub all over the chicken. Cover and refrigerate for 6 hours or overnight.

To make the sauce, combine all the ingredients in a bowl. Pour over 125 ml (4 fl oz/½ cup) boiling water, stir to combine and set aside. Soak some wooden skewers for 30 minutes.

Remove the chicken from the fridge 30 minutes before cooking. Thread the chicken onto skewers, three pieces on each.

Preheat the barbecue hotplate or grill to high. Cook the skewers for 8–10 minutes, or until cooked through, turning often.

Spoon the sauce over to serve.

COCONUT CHICKEN TENDERLOINS

Serves 4

This is kind of Indian, but then again the flavours are more typical of the Caribbean—lots of fragrant spice, coconut and tropical lime. Tenderloins are great as they don't have the fat of the thigh and don't tend to dry out either.

METHOD

Put the chicken in a large non-metallic dish.

Put the onion, parsley, coriander, cloves, cinnamon, lime juice and coconut milk in a food processor and process to a paste. Pour the marinade over the chicken and toss to cover the chicken in the marinade. Cover and refrigerate for 3–6 hours.

Remove the chicken from the fridge 30 minutes before cooking. Preheat the barbecue hotplate to high. Drizzle the olive oil onto the hotplate to grease. Shake any excess marinade off the chicken and put the tenderloins on the hotplate, making sure there is some space between each one. Cook for 8–10 minutes, turning often, until cooked through and the chicken is golden, tender and aromatic.

Arrange on a serving platter with the lime cheeks on the side. Sprinkle with the paprika and scatter over the coriander, if using.

INGREDIENTS

800 g (1 lb 12 oz) chicken tenderloins
1 onion, chopped
1 handful flat-leaf (Italian) parsley
1 handful coriander (cilantro) leaves
¼ teaspoon ground cloves
¼ teaspoon ground cinnamon
1 tablespoon lime juice
250 ml (9 fl oz/1 cup) coconut milk
2 tablespoons light olive oil
lime cheeks, to serve
½ teaspoon sweet paprika, to serve (optional)
coriander (cilantro) sprigs, to serve (optional)

CHINATOWN DUCK SHANKS

Serves 4

When I first saw the words duck and shank together I thought it must be a mistake, or a joke. After all isn't a shank part of the leg of a four-legged creature? I was thinking lamb. But, no. A shank is the part of the leg of any vertebrate. Anyway, lucky for me I live but 20 minutes from Australia's largest free-range duck farm. This means lots of whole ducks, livers, marylands and shanks.

INGREDIENTS

12 duck shanks
2 tablespoons hoisin sauce
2 tablespoons light soy sauce
2 tablespoons Chinese rice wine
2 star anise
2 drops cochineal (optional)
2 tablespoons honey
2 spring onions (scallions), thinly
    sliced on an angle
Chinese barbecue sauce (char siu),
    to serve

METHOD

Put the duck shanks into a dish with the hoisin sauce, soy sauce, rice wine, star anise and cochineal, if using, tossing the shanks around in the marinade. Cover and refrigerate for 24 hours, turning the duck every now and then.

Remove the duck from the fridge 30 minutes before cooking.

Preheat the barbecue hotplate and grill to medium and close the lid to create a hot-oven effect.

Remove the duck from the marinade. Sit the duck on a rack and sit the rack over a deep baking tray. Half fill the baking tray with water and sit on the barbecue, close the lid and cook for 30 minutes. Turn the duck shanks over and cook for another 30 minutes, or until golden. Brush the honey over the shanks and cook for another 10 minutes, turning the shanks and brushing each side with the honey until glistening and crisp.

Arrange the shanks on a serving platter and scatter over the spring onion. Serve with the Chinese barbecue sauce on the side.

CREOLE CHICKEN

Serves 4

This is a versatile one. The marinade and sauce would work really nicely with pork fillet or pork chop, rump steak or flank steak. I can even imagine it working beautifully with lamb.

METHOD

Put the chicken in a non-metallic dish or bowl. Put the onion, garlic, coriander stems, olive oil and vinegar in a food processor and process to a paste. Rub all over the chicken. Cover and refrigerate for 6 hours or overnight.

Remove the chicken from the fridge 30 minutes before cooking.

To make the sauce, put all the sauce ingredients in a small bowl, stirring to combine.

Preheat the barbecue grill or hotplate to high. Cook the chicken, skin side down, for 8–10 minutes. Turn over and cook for another 5 minutes, or until cooked through. Remove and allow to rest for 10 minutes.

Spoon the sauce over the hot chicken and serve with grilled corn and vine-ripened tomatoes, if desired.

INGREDIENTS

4 boneless chicken breasts,
    with skin on
1 onion, chopped
2 garlic cloves, chopped
1 tablespoon finely chopped
    coriander (cilantro) stems
2 tablespoons olive oil
2 tablespoons white wine vinegar

SAUCE

2 tablespoons olive oil
2 tablespoons lime juice
2 teaspoons ground cumin
2 garlic cloves, crushed
3 tablespoons chopped coriander
    (cilantro) leaves

CHICKEN LIVER SKEWERS WITH SICHUAN PEPPER SALT

Serves 2–4

I do like my Chinese food and the inspiration for this comes from a stir-fried chicken liver dish I had at a Chinese restaurant in Sydney. If you don't like livers then you would have turned the page already. But if you do, then you know exactly how I feel. Livers look less appetising when in a sauce. These ones are simply and quickly cooked on a very hot barbecue hotplate.

INGREDIENTS

1 teaspoon sichuan peppercorns
1 teaspoon sea salt
500 g (1 lb 2 oz) chicken livers
2 tablespoons balsamic vinegar
2 tablespoons light soy sauce
chargrilled orange cheeks, to serve

METHOD

Put the peppercorns and salt in a small frying pan over high heat. Cook until the peppercorns start to smoke, shaking the pan to ensure even cooking. Remove from the heat. Tip the salt and peppercorns into a bowl and allow to cool. Put into a spice grinder and grind until the mixture looks like fine, smoky-coloured salt. Tip into a bowl.

Trim and discard excess sinew and veins from the livers, trying not to break them up too much. Combine the livers in a non-metallic bowl with the vinegar and soy sauce. Set aside at room temperature for 30 minutes. Soak four bamboo skewers.

Thread the pieces of liver onto four skewers.

Preheat the barbecue hotplate to high and drizzle with olive oil to lightly grease.

Cook the livers for 2–3 minutes each side, until golden.

Sprinkle over the peppercorn and salt mix and serve with the chargrilled orange cheeks.

CHILLI YOGHURT CHICKEN

Serves 6

Don't you just love a good food memory? I remember my first banana fritter—yum. My first taste of coriander—odd and challenging. Then there is this combination of yoghurt and chicken I had at a cutting-edge café in the Blue Mountains, west of Sydney, in the early 1980s. I say cutting edge because the gals who ran this place were exploring flavours and ingredients ten years ahead of everyone else. At a time when much of the food scene was haute, teensy and uptight, they were doing big, bold and tasty food from Asia and the Middle East. They passed on this recipe to me.

METHOD

Combine the yoghurt, garlic, ginger, chilli powder and lemon juice in a large non-metallic bowl or dish. Add the chicken and toss to coat. Cover and refrigerate for 6 hours or overnight.

Remove from the fridge 30 minutes before cooking.

Preheat the barbecue hotplate to high. Drizzle a little of the olive oil onto the hotplate to grease. Put the chicken onto the hotplate and cook for 7–8 minutes, or until golden. Make sure the chicken sizzles the whole time. Turn over and cook for another 7–8 minutes, or until cooked through.

Serve with the lemon cheeks and rocket.

INGREDIENTS

130 g (4½ oz/½ cup) plain yoghurt
2 garlic cloves, crushed
½ teaspoon ground ginger
¼ teaspoon chilli powder
2 tablespoons lemon juice
6 boneless, skinless chicken thighs
light olive oil, for cooking
lemon cheeks, to serve
rocket (arugula) leaves, to serve

PIRI PIRI SPATCHCOCK

Serves 4

We have seen many fast-food franchises claiming to provide Portuguese flavoured grilled chicken. Some of it is good. According to the recipe title, my version makes a similar claim. It is not traditional, with the inclusion of Chinese chilli garlic sauce and shop-bought roasted red capsicum in the ingredient list. But I think it is very tasty and extremely easy.

PIRI PIRI MARINADE
300 g (10½ oz/1½ cups) chopped roasted red capsicum
4 tablespoons Chinese chilli garlic sauce
1½ tablespoons olive oil
1½ teaspoons ground cumin
1½ teaspoons fresh marjoram, plus extra, for serving

4 small chickens, about 500 g (1 lb 2 oz) each

METHOD
To make the piri piri marinade, put all the ingredients in a food processor and blend until smooth. Set aside.

Sit each chicken, breast side up, on a chopping board. Lay the palm of your hand on the top of the chicken to make stable. Insert a large knife into the cavity of the chicken and cut either side of the backbone. Remove and discard the backbone.

Flatten the chickens on the chopping board by firmly pressing down on the breastbone with the palm of your hand.

Put the chickens in a large dish or bowl and rub all over with two-thirds of the marinade. Put the remaining marinade in a bowl and refrigerate until needed. Cover the chicken and refrigerate for 3–6 hours or overnight, turning often.

Remove the chicken from the fridge 30 minutes before cooking.

Preheat the barbecue hotplate and grill to high and close the lid to create a hot-oven effect.

Sprinkle sea salt over the skin of the chicken. Lay the chicken, skin side down, on the hotplate, close the lid and cook for 5 minutes. Reduce the heat to medium–low and cook for another 10–15 minutes, until aromatic and the skin is dark golden. Turn over and cook for another 15 minutes, or until the chicken is cooked through. Allow to rest for 10–15 minutes.

Scatter with fresh marjoram leaves and serve with reserved marinade as a sauce.

SPICED QUAIL WITH VIETNAMESE LIME AND PEPPER DIPPING SAUCE

Serves 4

Every Vietnamese restaurant seems to have its own version of this quail. From what I can gather, it is probably marinated, then deep-fried. We can't do that here so I am going for grilling. And why not? It works perfectly well. The dipping sauce is zesty and peppery with a sherbety feel on the tongue.

METHOD

To make the lime and pepper sauce, combine all the ingredients in a small bowl and set aside.

Sit a quail on a chopping board, breast side up. Use a small sharp knife to insert into the cavity of the quail and cut either side of the backbone. Remove and discard the backbone. Open the quail to flatten on the chopping board, so it is butterflied. With the palm of your hand, press down on the breastbone to flatten. Cut each quail lengthways in half to give 16 pieces. Put the quail into a large bowl or dish with the rice bran oil, five-spice and sea salt, tossing the quail around to coat in the mixture. Set aside for 1 hour.

Preheat the barbecue hotplate to medium. Cover the hotplate with a sheet of baking paper. Lay the quail, skin side down, on the paper, close the lid and cook for 10 minutes, until the quail is aromatic and the skin crispy. Turn the quail over and cook for another 4–5 minutes, until the quail is golden, aromatic and cooked through.

Serve the quail with the lime and pepper sauce in a bowl on the side, and the lime wedges.

LIME AND PEPPER SAUCE

3 tablespoons lime juice
½ teaspoon ground white pepper
½ teaspoon caster (superfine) sugar

8 quail
1 tablespoon rice bran oil
½ teaspoon Chinese five-spice
1 teaspoon sea salt
lime wedges, to serve

KERALAN CHICKEN

Serves 4

Keralan cuisine is much less complex and full-on than in other parts of India. And by full-on I mean heavy and rich. This is a very simple barbecued chicken dish. It would also work really well with a maryland (drumstick and thigh on the bone), but do remember it would need a longer cooking time.

INGREDIENTS

4 boneless chicken breasts,
   with skin on
3 tablespoons lemon juice
2 garlic cloves, finely chopped
1 tablespoon finely grated ginger
1 small onion, chopped
¼ teaspoon ground turmeric
1 teaspoon ground cumin
1 teaspoon paprika
¼ teaspoon chilli powder
vegetable oil, for cooking
4 slices of flat bread or naan bread,
   sliced tomato, sliced red onion,
   coriander (cilantro) sprigs,
   plain yoghurt and lemon
   wedges, to serve

METHOD

Put the chicken in a ceramic dish. Put the lemon juice, garlic, ginger, onion, turmeric, cumin, paprika and chilli powder in a food processor and process to a smooth paste. Pour over the chicken. Roll the chicken around to coat in the marinade. Cover and refrigerate for 6 hours or overnight.

Remove the chicken from the fridge 30 minutes before cooking.

Preheat the barbecue hotplate to high. Drizzle a little vegetable oil over the hotplate to lightly grease.

Put the chicken, skin side down, on the hotplate and cook for 8–10 minutes, or until the skin is golden. Turn the heat to low and turn the chicken over. Close the lid and cook for 10 minutes, or until the chicken is cooked through. Remove and cover loosely with foil to rest for about 10 minutes before carving.

Cook the flat bread on the barbecue until warmed through and a little charred. Serve slices of the chicken on the flat bread and top with the sliced tomato, red onion and coriander sprigs, with the yoghurt and lemon wedges on the side.

LEMON, BALSAMIC AND GINGER WINGS

Serves 4

Okay, now this will sound odd. You are putting the chicken on a cold barbecue hotplate. This means your hotplate should be clean. But this is a good way to cook chicken wings. They are a thick, bony mass and often are overcooked on the outside before cooking all the way through. This method ensures even cooking.

METHOD

Chop the wing tip off each wing and discard. Cut between the joint to get two bits of chicken from each wing. Put the chicken into a large non-metallic bowl or dish. Combine the vinegar, lemon juice, olive oil, ginger, garlic and cayenne pepper and pour over the chicken. Use your hands to toss it all together, cover and refrigerate for 3–6 hours or overnight.

Remove from the fridge 30 minutes before cooking. Do not turn the barbecue on but lay your wings onto the clean, cold hotplate. Sprinkle sea salt generously all over the chicken. Now turn the heat on to high, close the lid and cook for 12–15 minutes, or until golden. After several minutes you will hear the chicken start to sizzle. Turn the chicken over and cook for another 5 minutes, or until cooked through. Serve with the lemon cheeks, extra salt and freshly ground black pepper.

INGREDIENTS

12 chicken wings
125 ml (4 fl oz/½ cup) balsamic
    vinegar
125 ml (4 fl oz/½ cup) lemon juice
2 tablespoons light olive oil
2 tablespoons finely grated ginger
2 garlic cloves, crushed
¼ teaspoon cayenne pepper
lemon cheeks, to serve

SLOW-COOKED SHANTUNG CHICKEN

Serves 4

If you're a fan of barbecued chicken from the local takeaway you are bound to love this. The sauce here is a classic balance of salt, sour, sweet and spice. It takes the humble chook to another level.

INGREDIENTS
1 large chicken, about 1.8 kg (4 lb)
2 tablespoons sesame oil
2 tablespoons light soy sauce
1 tablespoon lemon juice

SHANTUNG SAUCE
2 tablespoons light soy sauce
2 tablespoons rice vinegar
2 teaspoons caster (superfine) sugar
½ teaspoon sea salt
2 large red chillies, thinly sliced
1 small bunch coriander (cilantro),
    roughly chopped

METHOD
Sit the chicken, breast side up, on a chopping board. Use a long, sharp knife to reach into the cavity of the chicken and cut either side of the backbone. Remove and discard the backbone.

Flatten the chicken on the chopping board and press down on the breastbone with the palm of your hand to butterfly.

Put the chicken in a large dish. Combine the sesame oil, light soy sauce and lemon juice in a small bowl. Pour over the chicken, cover and refrigerate for 3 hours.

Remove the chicken from the fridge 1 hour before cooking.

Preheat the barbecue hotplate and grill to low and close the lid to create a hot-oven effect.

Take a 'V'-shaped barbecue rack and turn it over so it is now an upside down 'V'. Put the chicken on the grill rack, with the breast bone in the centre and reserve the marinade. Sit the grill rack on the hotplate, close the lid and cook on low heat for 1½–2¼ hours, basting every 15 minutes with the reserved marinade, or until the chicken is golden brown and tender enough to remove the flesh with a fork. Remove the chicken to a serving platter.

To make the shantung sauce, combine all the ingredients in a bowl and pour over the warm chicken. Serve with steamed Asian greens, if desired.

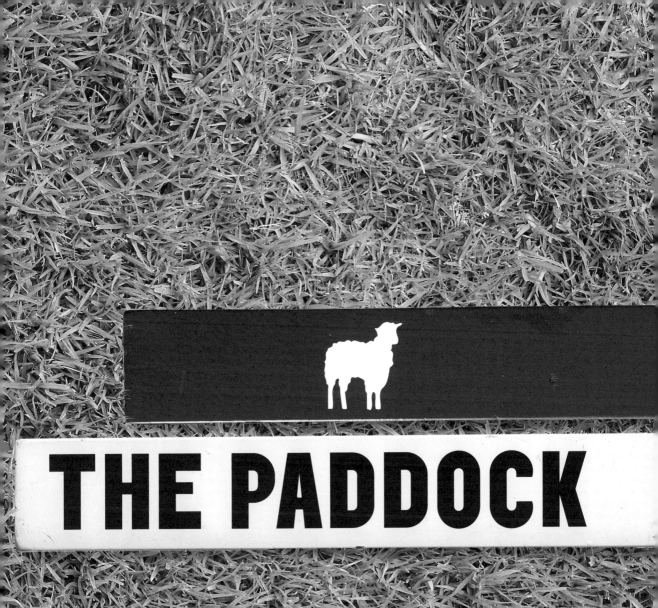

THE PADDOCK

BARBECUING: RAW MEAT ON HOT METAL. POSSIBLY THE MOST primitive way of cooking, but we still do it today. Barbecuing brings us back to the most basic of basics. Applying heat to cook our food. And red meat may well be the food we cook and enjoy most on a barbecue.

Creatures from the paddock include beef, lamb, pork—with a couple of others, like venison and veal, thrown in for a bit of variety.

I had to hold myself back from monopolising the whole chapter with cuts of meat I love most—rump steak and leg of lamb. Nothing could be better than a whopping big slab of rump ever so briefly immersed in a marinade of soy sauce infused with the holy trinity of Chinese flavourings—ginger, garlic and shallots. Or marinated in Spanish sherry with garlic and bay leaf. Cooked to medium–rare over a lick of a flame. Heaven!

Or throw a butterflied leg of lamb in a marinade of yoghurt spiked with aromatic and heady Indian spices. Let magic do its work and transform the barbecued leg of lamb into a flavour fantasy. Paradise!

With meat I lean towards several cuisines for flavour inspiration— Indian, Greek, Middle Eastern and North African. They have it down to a fine art: lots and lots of lemon and oregano; garlic and olive oil; cumin and coriander; mint and parsley. Pressed for time? Flavour inexpensive mince with some of these aromatics. Roll the mixture between two wet palms and you have kefta, meatballs or rissoles! Ready to be cooked on your grill in no time at all.

And my crush on Spanish flavours is neither fleeting nor fickle. I continue my love of olive oil, smoked paprika, bay leaves, sherry vinegar. And lots of garlic. All these flavours work so well with beef, pork and lamb.

Use terrific cuts of pork; lean and tender. Or go the whole hog and cook a big hunk of pork belly or shoulder until tender and unctuous. Spice up pork with chilli, any colour, any size, thank you. Or garlic, lemongrass and coriander.

Treat your barbecue as an oven. Preheat all the burners to high and close the lid to create a hot-oven effect. Ready to roast or slow cook your favourite cut.

Let's not overlook posh cuts of meat like sirloin (New York cut) and beef fillet—they require little more than a flavoured butter, a simple sauce or a sprinkling of something special. They don't need over fussing in the form of marinades or sauces.

With our favourite steaks it's about a few simple things. Let the meat come to room temperature before putting anywhere near a flame. Season well. Once on the barbecue, turn as little as possible. And let it rest.

PORK AND VEAL MEATBALLS

Serves 6-8

We make heaps of these at our tapas restaurant. They are so good for a few reasons. They can be made a day in advance, and the flavour will actually benefit from doing so. You can eat these 'dry' as in this recipe or serve them in a very simple tomato-based sauce with some bread on the side.

INGREDIENTS

500 g (1 lb 2 oz) minced (ground) pork
500 g (1 lb 2 oz) minced (ground) veal
60 g (2¼ oz/1 cup) fresh breadcrumbs
1 red onion, grated
1 garlic clove, crushed
1 teaspoon ground cinnamon
1 teaspoon ground cumin
½ teaspoon chilli flakes
1 teaspoon dried oregano
2 teaspoons smoked paprika
1 egg
light olive oil, for cooking

METHOD

Combine all the ingredients except the olive oil in a bowl, using your hands to mix really well. Pick up handfuls of the mixture and firmly throw back into the bowl or onto a clean work surface. This helps to tenderise the meat and remove any air. Use wet hands to roll the mixture into golf ball sizes and flatten each ball slightly to make a disc.

Preheat the barbecue hotplate or grill to medium and drizzle with the olive oil to lightly grease. Cook the meatballs for 8 minutes, turning every minute and gently pressing down with a spatula, until golden and aromatic.

LAMB WITH GREEN OLIVE SALSA

Serves 6

Lamb cuts from young animals are perfect for quick cooking—backstrap, fillet, loin chops, cutlets and medallions. But the leg may well be the thing we most associate with lamb. Leaving the skin and fat on allows the meat to cook without burning.

METHOD

As the lamb will be thicker at one end, make several deep cuts into the thicker part to allow more even cooking. Put the lamb in a large ceramic dish or bowl with the wine, lemon juice, olive oil, rosemary and garlic. Set aside at room temperature for 2–3 hours or cover and refrigerate for up to a day, turning the lamb often.

To make the salsa, put all the ingredients in a food processor and process to a paste. Set aside.

Remove the lamb from the fridge 1 hour before cooking.

Preheat the barbecue hotplate and grill to high and close the lid to create a hot-oven effect. Drizzle a little olive oil on the hotplate to grease. Remove the lamb from the marinade, reserving the marinade. Cook the lamb skin side down on the hotplate for 8–10 minutes, or until the skin is browned. Turn the lamb over and cook for another 5 minutes. Put the lamb on a 'V'-shaped barbecue rack and spoon over the marinade. Reduce the heat to medium. Sit the rack on the hotplate, close the lid and cook for 20–25 minutes, or until cooked as desired. Remove the lamb to a large serving plate, cover loosely with foil, and rest for 15–20 minutes.

Thickly slice the lamb and arrange on a serving platter with the green olive salsa spooned over. Serve with the Sicilian grilled vegetable salad.

INGREDIENTS

1 small leg of lamb, about 1.6 kg
  (3 lb 8 oz), butterflied
125 ml (4 fl oz/½ cup) dry
  white wine
3 tablespoons lemon juice
3 tablespoons olive oil, plus extra,
  for cooking
1 handful rosemary sprigs
10–12 garlic cloves, peeled
  and crushed
Sicilian grilled vegetable salad, to
  serve (see p 188)

GREEN OLIVE SALSA

175 g (6 oz/1 cup) green olives,
  pitted
6 baby gherkins (cornichons)
2 large handfuls flat-leaf (Italian)
  parsley
2 large handfuls mint
2 garlic cloves, chopped
3 anchovy fillets
3 tablespoons lemon juice
125 ml (4 fl oz/½ cup) olive oil

PORK SHOULDER WITH VINEGAR, GARLIC AND SPICE

Serves 6–8

You know, we often think that we need to eat meat as soon as it comes off the barbecue. And most things, like a good steak, may well taste better when eaten straight after cooking. But then there are some things which you just have to rest, like whole chickens and big, beefy cuts of meat. And then there is a recipe like this, which is just as tasty cold as it is hot.

INGREDIENTS

1.5 kg (3 lb 5 oz) pork shoulder, skin on
375 ml (13 fl oz/1½ cups) red wine vinegar
6 garlic cloves, lightly crushed
2 bay leaves
2 teaspoons allspice
1 teaspoon sea salt
1 teaspoon smoked paprika
1 teaspoon cayenne pepper

METHOD

Sit the pork, skin side up, in a non-metallic dish. Combine the remaining ingredients in a bowl and pour over the pork. Cover and refrigerate for 24 hours, turning the pork every 6 hours or so. Remove the pork from the marinade 1 hour before cooking.

Preheat the barbecue hotplate and grill to high and close the lid to create a hot-oven effect. Sit the pork, skin side up, on a cooking rack set over a deep-sided baking tray half filled with water. Put the tray on the hotplate, close the lid and cook for 30 minutes. Turn the heat down to low and cook for another 1¼ minutes, topping up the tray with water as it evaporates.

Remove the pork to a serving plate, cover loosely with foil and allow to rest for 15–20 minutes before carving.

BEEF RIB EYE FILLET WITH HORSERADISH BUTTER

Serves 4

This is a good example of how meat can benefit from sitting at room temperature before cooking and from resting after cooking. Rib eye does not require much cooking. This means if you cook it directly from the fridge it will still be cold in the centre. It doesn't generally have much fat so if overcooked it will be dry and if not rested it will be tough. Basically, this cut deserves a little respect.

METHOD

To make the horseradish butter, put all the ingredients in a food processor and process until well combined. Lay a sheet of plastic wrap on a work surface. Put spoonfuls of the butter along the centre of the plastic, then firmly wrap and form into a log about 2 cm (¾ in) wide. Refrigerate for 2–3 hours, or until firm.

Rub the beef all over with the salt and pepper and set aside at room temperature for 1–2 hours.

Preheat the barbecue hotplate to medium and close the lid to create a hot-oven effect. Drizzle the olive oil over the hotplate to grease. Put the fillet on the hotplate, cover and cook for 5 minutes. Give the beef a quarter turn and cook for another 5 minutes. Repeat twice more so the beef is well browned on all sides. Wrap the beef loosely in foil and sit on the hot barbecue lid for 15 minutes. Remove and allow to rest for 15 minutes, wrapped in the foil. Thickly slice and serve on a platter with slices of the butter on top and oven-baked potato chips on the side, if desired.

HORSERADISH BUTTER

125 g (4½ oz) unsalted butter, softened to room temperature
1 tablespoon finely grated fresh horseradish
2 teaspoons Worcestershire sauce
1 garlic clove, crushed
1 tablespoon finely chopped spring onion (scallion)
1 tablespoon small salted capers, rinsed and well drained
2 anchovy fillets
2 tablespoons finely chopped flat-leaf (Italian) parsley

750–800 g (1 lb 10 oz–1 lb 12 oz) rib eye beef fillet
1 teaspoon sea salt
1 teaspoon freshly ground black pepper
1 tablespoon olive oil

CHAR SIU LAMB WRAPS

Serves 4

You may not associate cumin with Chinese flavours. In the north and west of China, lamb and wheat is abundant and dominates the cooking there. So you find lots of barbecued lamb flavoured with chilli and cumin and served with steamed buns and breads. Very nice.

INGREDIENTS

2 large lamb backstrap fillets,
    about 400 g (14 oz) each
2 teaspoons sesame oil
2 garlic cloves, finely chopped
2 teaspoons chilli flakes
2 teaspoons ground cumin
3 tablespoons Chinese barbecue
    sauce (char siu), plus extra,
    for serving
4 soft tortillas or burritos
4 spring onions (scallions),
    thinly sliced on the angle
2 Lebanese (short) cucumbers,
    halved lengthways and sliced

METHOD

Put the lamb in a bowl with the sesame oil, garlic, chilli and cumin. Toss the lamb around to coat all over with the marinade. Cover and set aside at room temperature for a couple of hours or cover and refrigerate for 3–6 hours, removing from the fridge 1 hour before cooking.

Preheat the barbecue hotplate to high.

Put the lamb on the hotplate and cook for 2 minutes. Turn over and cook for another 2 minutes. Brush the lamb with the barbecue sauce and turn. Continue to baste and turn the lamb, using all the remaining sauce for 4–5 minutes. Remove the lamb to a chopping board and cover loosely with foil for 5 minutes.

Slice the lamb. Spread a little of the extra char siu sauce down the centre of each tortilla. Top with sliced lamb, spring onion and cucumber. Roll up each tortilla and serve.

CHUNKY LAMB LEG STEAKS

Serves 4

Depending on how your butcher bones the leg, or how it is sold in the supermarket, I am hoping you can get four 'steaks' of equal size from the leg. If not, don't stress out. If the lamb leg is thin in parts, cut into smaller portions.

INGREDIENTS

1 small boned leg of lamb, about
    1 kg (2 lb 4 oz)
2 teaspoons ground cumin
1 teaspoon ground turmeric
2 teaspoons sea salt
70 g (2½ oz/¼ cup) plain yoghurt
2 onions, chopped
1 handful coriander leaves
    and stems
2 tablespoons finely grated ginger
2 garlic cloves, chopped
1 teaspoon garam masala

METHOD

Cut the lamb into four steaks, about 2 cm (¾ in) thick and put into a bowl with the cumin, turmeric and sea salt. Toss the lamb around to coat evenly in the spices and set aside.

Put the yoghurt, onion, coriander, ginger and garlic in a food processor and process to a paste. Spoon over the lamb and stir well to combine. Cover and set aside at room temperature for 2–3 hours, or refrigerate for 6 hours or overnight.

Remove the steaks from the fridge 1 hour before cooking.

Preheat the barbecue grill to medium. Cook the steaks for 5 minutes each side. Sprinkle over the garam masala and quickly turn the steaks on the grill for a few seconds each side so the spices cook and are aromatic.

VEAL AND EGGPLANT WITH LEMON DRESSING

Serves 4

This one has casual, al fresco entertaining stamped all over it. It will keep you busy on the barbie for but a short while. More time to enjoy other social activities.

METHOD

To make the lemon dressing, whisk the mustard, salt and lemon juice in a small bowl. Slowly add the olive oil, whisking constantly until thick. Set aside.

Put the veal, sea salt, chilli flakes, olive oil and some freshly ground black pepper in a bowl, tossing the veal around to coat in the mixture. Set aside at room temperature for 1–2 hours.

Preheat the barbecue grill to high. Lightly brush each side of the eggplant with some olive oil and cook on the grill for 3–4 minutes each side, so the eggplant is tender and slightly charred. Transfer to a serving plate.

Preheat the barbecue hotplate to high. Cook the veal for just 30 seconds each side. Randomly stack slices of veal and eggplant drizzled with the dressing. Scatter over the parsley to serve.

LEMON DRESSING

1 teaspoon dijon mustard
½ teaspoon sea salt
1 tablespoon lemon juice
3 tablespoons olive oil

4 veal schnitzels, about 150 g
    (5½ oz) each
1 teaspoon sea salt
½ teaspoon chilli flakes
2 tablespoons light olive oil
1 eggplant (aubergine), cut into
    1 cm (½ in) slices
1 handful roughly chopped flat-leaf
    (Italian) parsley, to serve

HAGEN'S PORK NECK

Serves 8

I was a tad envious when my friend Hagen made this. It looked like it was not going to work at all. This big piece of meat was surely going to burn before it had a chance of being cooked through. But cooked to perfection it was, and extremely tasty too. Thanks for the inspiration mate!

METHOD

Put the pork in a flat ceramic dish.

Put the remaining ingredients in a food processor and process to a smooth paste. Rub all over the pork, cover and set aside at room temperature for 2–3 hours, or refrigerate overnight.

Remove from the fridge 2 hours before cooking.

Preheat the barbecue hotplate to medium. Drizzle a little vegetable oil on the hotplate to lightly grease and then add the pork.

Cook the pork for 8–10 minutes, turning often until well browned all over.

Put the pork on a 'V'-shaped barbecue rack. Sit the rack on the hotplate, close the lid and cook for 1 hour. Allow to rest for 20–30 minutes before carving.

INGREDIENTS

2 kg (4 lb 8 oz) pork neck, butterflied to a thickness of 3–4 cm (1¼–1½ in)

1 bunch coriander (cilantro) leaves, stems and roots, finely chopped

1 garlic bulb, cloves peeled

12 large red chillies, chopped

1 teaspoon sea salt

3 tablespoons honey

3 tablespoons dark soy sauce

3 tablespoons black rice vinegar

vegetable oil, for cooking

CURRIED LEG OF LAMB

Serves 6–8

The ingredient list here is about as lengthy as you will find in this book, or with my recipes in general for that matter. Sometimes with Indian flavours this is unavoidable for an authentic result. A curry really is just a blend or combination of spices. If you have any shop-bought curry powder or paste have a look at the ingredient list and you'll see what I mean. Making your own though is one sure way to ensure a more flavoursome, pungent and aromatic curry.

INGREDIENTS

1 leg of lamb, about 1.5 kg
   (3 lb 5 oz), boned and butterflied
3 tablespoons lemon juice
2 tablespoons olive oil
½ teaspoon chilli powder
2 tablespoons sea salt
pomegranate seeds, to serve
   (optional)

SPICE PASTE

1 teaspoon saffron threads
1 onion, chopped
2 garlic cloves, chopped
1 tablespoon finely grated ginger
2 teaspoons black mustard seeds
2 whole cloves
4 cardamom pods
1 teaspoon coriander seeds
1 teaspoon cumin seeds
1 teaspoon fennel seeds
130 g (4½ oz/½ cup) plain yoghurt
2 tablespoons pomegranate
   molasses

METHOD

Put the lamb in a large flat dish. Combine the lemon juice, olive oil, chilli powder and sea salt in a small bowl and pour over the lamb. Cover and set aside for about 1 hour. Do not refrigerate.

To make the spice paste, put the saffron in a bowl with 60 ml (2 fl oz/¼ cup) boiling water. Leave for 10 minutes, until the water is a vibrant saffron colour. Put all the remaining ingredients in a food processor, including the saffron water. Process for several seconds then scrape down the side of the processor with a spatula. Repeat several more times. Pour the paste over the lamb. Toss the lamb around so it is completely covered with the spice paste. Cover and leave at room temperature for 2–3 hours, or refrigerate overnight.

Remove the lamb from the fridge 1 hour before cooking.

Preheat the barbecue hotplate and grill to high and close the lid to create a hot-oven effect.

Sit the lamb on a 'V'-shaped barbecue rack. Sit the rack on the hotplate, close the lid and cook for 20 minutes. Reduce the heat to medium and cook for another 20 minutes.

Remove the lamb to a large serving plate, cover loosely with foil and allow to rest for 20 minutes before carving. Serve with the pomegranate seeds, if desired.

LEMONGRASS, PEPPER AND CORIANDER PORK SKEWERS

Serves 4

In Vietnam and much of the cooking of Southeast Asia, pork is often used with sweet, salty and sour flavours. Here, barbecued pork mince cooks to a charred sweetness complemented by the fragrant lemongrass.

METHOD

To make the nuoc cham, combine all the ingredients in a bowl. Set aside.

Put the pork, chopped lemongrass, sugar, fish sauce, coriander and black pepper in a food processor and process until well combined. Scrape into a bowl. Pick the mince up and firmly throw it back into the bowl or onto a clean work surface to remove any air.

Divide the mixture into eight equal portions. Using wet hands, wrap a ball of the mixture around a stalk of lemongrass. Repeat with the remaining lemongrass and pork. The pork mixture can be made to this stage up to a day in advance.

Preheat the barbecue grill to high. Brush the oil over the pork mixture and cook on the barbecue for 8–10 minutes, turning every minute until golden and cooked through.

To serve, wrap the pork in the lettuce leaves and spoon over the nuoc cham.

NUOC CHAM

4 small red chillies, finely chopped
2 garlic cloves, finely chopped
2 teaspoons sugar
1 tablespoon rice vinegar
125 ml (4 fl oz/½ cup) fish sauce

500 g (1 lb 2 oz) minced (ground) pork
2 lemongrass stalks, white part only, finely chopped
1 teaspoon caster (superfine) sugar
1 tablespoon fish sauce
2 tablespoons chopped coriander (cilantro) roots
1 teaspoon freshly ground black pepper
8 lemongrass stalks, about 15 cm (6 in) long
vegetable oil, for cooking
lettuce leaves, to serve

VEAL AND PROVOLONE INVOLTINI

Serves 4

Think of involtini as a roll or a log. Provolone is a very tasty, firm Italian cheese that melts to a very gooey goodness. This, with the pancetta, really complements the mildly flavoured, yet tender, veal.

INGREDIENTS
400 g (14 oz) veal backstrap fillet
1 egg, lightly beaten
1 tablespoon finely chopped
    flat-leaf (Italian) parsley
1 tablespoon finely chopped
    rosemary
4 slices pancetta
75 g (2½ oz) provolone cheese,
    thinly sliced
2 tablespoons olive oil

METHOD
Cut the veal into four equal-sized portions. Put the veal between two layers of plastic wrap or baking paper and pound until very thin.

Combine the egg, parsley and rosemary in a bowl then brush over the top side of each slice of veal. Top each piece of veal with a slice of pancetta and a layer of provolone.

Firmly roll up the veal into a log and tie with cooking string. Lay the veal rolls in a tray and rub all over with the olive oil. Season with salt and freshly ground black pepper and set aside for 30 minutes.

Preheat the barbecue grill to high. Cook the rolls for 8 minutes, turning every 2 minutes, until golden. Remove and rest for 5 minutes. Slice each roll into 3–4 pieces to serve. Serve with a simple rocket and parmesan salad, if desired.

SIRLOIN STEAKS WITH CHIMICHURRI BUTTER

Serves 4

Sirloin is also known as a New York cut. I reckon it is best appreciated when cut quite thick, leaving a nice bit of fat along one side. Sirloin and rump are my two fave cuts of steak. And the butter used in this recipe would go nicely with rump too. Chimichurri is South American in origin, probably Argentinian. It is a highly addictive, herb-filled, vinegar-spiked sauce.

METHOD

To make the chimichurri butter, put all the ingredients in a food processor and process until well combined. Lay a sheet of plastic wrap on a work surface. Put spoonfuls of the butter along the centre of the plastic, then firmly wrap and form into a log. Refrigerate for 2–3 hours, or until firm.

Remove the steaks from the fridge 1–2 hours before cooking. Brush with the olive oil, sprinkle a little sea salt on the top side of each steak and leave for 5–10 minutes.

Preheat the barbecue hotplate or grill to medium–high. Put the seasoned side of the steaks on the hotplate or grill and sprinkle a little sea salt on the top side of the steaks. Cook for 4 minutes. Turn over and cook for another 3 minutes. Remove from the hotplate, cover with foil and rest for 5 minutes.

Slice the butter and serve on the hot steaks. Serve with chargrilled corn, if desired.

CHIMICHURRI BUTTER

1 handful coriander (cilantro) leaves
1 handful flat-leaf (Italian) parsley
½ teaspoon dried Greek oregano
2 garlic cloves, crushed
2 tablespoons red wine vinegar
125 g (4½ oz) unsalted butter, softened to room temperature

4 sirloin steaks
olive oil, for cooking

HAND-MADE PORK AND FENNEL SAUSAGES

Serves 4-6

These are not really a true sausage as they have no casing. But they take the shape of a sausage and taste as good as. The combination of pork, fennel and chilli flakes is very southern Italian where sausages are traditionally cooked on a grill in a large coil or spiral shape.

INGREDIENTS

1 kg (2 lb 4 oz) minced (ground) pork neck
1 teaspoon chilli flakes
1 tablespoon rice flour
1 tablespoon fennel seeds
1 teaspoon sea salt
8 garlic cloves, crushed
3 tablespoons finely chopped flat-leaf (Italian) parsley, plus extra, to serve
25 g (1 oz/¼ cup) finely grated pecorino cheese
olive oil, for cooking
chargrilled lemon wedges, to serve

METHOD

Use your hands to combine all the ingredients, except the olive oil and the lemon wedges, in a bowl. Pick the mixture up and firmly throw it back into the bowl or onto a clean work surface to remove any air.

Using wet hands, roll ¼ cup portions of the mixture into little sausages, about 10 cm (4 in) long.

Preheat the barbecue hotplate to high and lightly brush with some olive oil to grease. Cook the sausages for 4–5 minutes each side, until well browned and just cooked through. Scatter over the extra parsley and serve with the lemon wedges on the side.

ROAST BEEF FILLET WITH PAPRIKA MAYONNAISE

Serves 6

Here is a recipe from my old catering days. These beef fillets could be made in advance, grilled and just left to sit for a short while before being sliced to serve. Ready when you are. The prosciutto wrapped around the beef is cooked crisp, imparting even more flavour on the tender cut of beef.

METHOD

Trim the beef of any fat and sinew. Cut the garlic into thin slivers. Make incisions all over the beef and slip in the garlic slivers. Lay the beef fillet in a bowl and pour over the sherry. Set aside at room temperature for 2 hours, or cover and refrigerate for several hours or overnight, turning the beef every now and then.

Remove the beef from the fridge 1–2 hours before cooking.

Lay the slices of prosciutto, side by side, on a work surface.

Remove the beef from the sherry, draining well. Lay the beef fillet on the prosciutto and put the bay leaves on the beef. Wrap the beef and bay leaves up in the prosciutto. Secure with cooking string.

To make the paprika mayonnaise, combine all the ingredients in a small bowl and set aside.

Preheat the barbecue hotplate to medium. Lay the beef on the hotplate, close the lid and cook the beef for 20 minutes with the lid on, turning every 5 minutes. Turn the barbecue off and wrap the beef in foil. Sit the beef on the hot barbecue lid for 10 minutes. Remove from the lid, leave wrapped in foil and rest for another 10 minutes. Thickly slice, remove the bay leaves and serve with the paprika mayonnaise.

INGREDIENTS

1.5 kg (3 lb 5 oz) beef fillet
8 garlic cloves
500 ml (17 fl oz/2 cups) Spanish sherry
200 g (7 oz) thinly sliced prosciutto (about 10–12 slices)
8 fresh bay leaves
1 tablespoon olive oil

PAPRIKA MAYONNAISE

185 ml (6 fl oz/¾ cup) good quality mayonnaise
1 garlic clove, crushed
½ teaspoon Spanish paprika
2 teaspoons lemon juice

VENISON WITH REDCURRANT JELLY AND SOUR CREAM

Serves 4

My family generally opts for the more traditional fare at Christmas, despite the scorching heat of the Australian summer. However, I like to mix it up a bit and this recipe finds the perfect balance between traditional and contemporary.

INGREDIENTS

580 ml (20¼ fl oz/2⅓ cups) red wine, preferably Australian shiraz, reduced from 600 ml (21 fl oz)

125 ml (4 fl oz/½ cup) red wine vinegar, reduced from 150 ml (5 fl oz)

1 bay leaf

1 onion, peeled and cut in half

1 carrot, peeled and chopped

2 garlic cloves, lightly crushed

1 kg (2 lb 4 oz) venison fillet

2 tablespoons freshly ground black pepper

olive oil, for cooking

160 g (5½ oz/½ cup) redcurrant jelly

125 g (4½ oz/½ cup) sour cream

1 handful chervil, to serve

METHOD

Put the red wine, vinegar, bay leaf, onion, carrot and garlic in a large non-metallic bowl or dish. Add the venison, ensuring it is submerged in the marinade, and refrigerate for at least 24 hours.

Remove the venison from the marinade, draining well, and rub the venison all over with the pepper. Set aside at room temperature for 1–2 hours before cooking.

Preheat the barbecue hotplate to high. Lightly brush the hotplate with some olive oil to grease. Put the fillet on the hotplate and sprinkle with sea salt. Close the lid and cook for 20 minutes, turning every 5 minutes. Wrap the meat in foil and turn the barbecue off. Lay the wrapped meat on the hot barbecue lid for 10 minutes. Remove from the lid, leave wrapped in foil and rest for another 10 minutes.

Just before serving roughly combine the redcurrant jelly and the sour cream. Thickly slice the venison and serve with the redcurrant–sour cream mixture. Scatter over the chervil to serve.

CHORIZO WITH APPLE CIDER VINEGAR

Serves 4

Enjoy this recipe tapas style, with some nice bread and a salad of crisp lettuce, tomato, red onion and Spanish olives on the side. Bump up the quantity to make as much as you like, cooking the chorizo off in batches as the troops demand more.

METHOD

Finely slice the chorizo on an angle and toss the slices around in a bowl with the olive oil.

Preheat the barbecue hotplate to high. Tip the chorizo onto the hotplate and spread them around. Cook for 2–3 minutes, turn over and cook for another couple of minutes until they begin to crisp up. Pour the vinegar over the chorizo and, as it sizzles, quickly toss the chorizo on the hotplate.

Put the chorizo on a serving plate and serve sprinkled with coriander and with the lemon wedges and sliced baguette on the side.

INGREDIENTS

500 g (1 lb 2 oz) smoked chorizo
1 tablespoon olive oil
3 tablespoons apple cider vinegar
1 handful finely chopped coriander
    (cilantro) leaves, (optional)
lemon wedges, to serve, (optional)
sliced baguette, to serve

LAMB FILLET WITH HERBS AND PISTACHIOS

Serves 4

Marinades for lamb can afford to have a bite in the form of vinegars and mustards without being overbearing. This recipe also includes a wonderfully tangy pomegranate molasses. Hailing from the Middle East, a little bit of this stuff goes a long way.

INGREDIENTS
2 lamb backstrap fillets, about 260 g (9¼ oz) each
2 tablespoons finely chopped flat-leaf (Italian) parsley
1 tablespoon finely snipped chives
1 teaspoon finely chopped thyme
2 thinly sliced French shallots (eschalots)
2 garlic cloves, finely chopped
3 tablespoons red wine vinegar
1 tablespoon dijon mustard
3 tablespoons olive oil, plus extra, for cooking
2 tablespoons pistachio nuts, roughly chopped
1 tablespoon pomegranate molasses
crusty bread, to serve

METHOD
Put the lamb in a dish. Combine the parsley, chives, thyme, shallots, garlic, vinegar, mustard and olive oil in a food processor. Process to a rough paste. Spoon the mixture over the lamb. Roll the lamb around in the dish so it is coated all over in the marinade. Cover and refrigerate for 3–6 hours.

Remove the lamb from the fridge 1 hour before cooking.

Preheat the barbecue hotplate to high and lightly brush with some olive oil to grease. Put the lamb on the hotplate and pour over the marinade. Sprinkle with sea salt. Cook for 3 minutes each side. Remove, cover with foil and rest for 5 minutes.

Thickly slice the lamb and arrange on a serving plate. Top with the pistachios and drizzle with the pomegranate molasses. Serve with the crusty bread.

SPANISH RUMP STEAK

Serves 4

This is a very broad title. After all, Spain is a big place and Spanish cooking uses many flavours. But I do find myself drawn to smoked paprika and sherry, two of the big-boys of flavour in Spanish cooking. They are so intense and unique.

INGREDIENTS
4 rump steaks, about 200 g (7 oz) each and about 1.5 cm (⅝ in) thick
6 garlic cloves, finely chopped
2 bay leaves
250 ml (9 fl oz/1 cup) Spanish or dry sherry
2 tablespoons olive oil

METHOD
Put the steaks in a flat dish. Combine the garlic, bay leaves, sherry and olive oil in a bowl and pour over the steaks. Turn the steaks over a couple of times to coat in the marinade. Cover and refrigerate for at least 6 hours or overnight, turning the steaks every now and then.

Remove the steak from the fridge 1 hour prior to cooking.

Preheat the barbecue hotplate to high. When the hotplate is smoking hot, add the steaks and cook for 4 minutes, turn over and cook for another 3 minutes.

Rest the steaks for 5 minutes before serving.

BRUNCH CROQUES

Serves 4

A croque monsieur (or madame for that matter) has become an urbane brunch item. Yes, it can have béchamel, but why would you bother? Traditionally, it's really nothing more than a toasted ham and cheese sandwich enjoyed by peasant workers in France at some point in the past. But folks, I would insist on using the best ham you can and only go for gruyère. Nothing else cuts it with this perfect hangover cure.

METHOD

Put the bread on a work surface and spread the top side of each slice using about half of the butter.

On the other side of the bread, evenly spread the mustard. Put a slice of ham on top and divide the cheese over the ham. Put a slice of bread, butter side down, on top and spread with some of the remaining butter.

Preheat the barbecue hotplate to medium. Put the sandwich, buttered side down, on the hotplate. Spread any remaining butter on the top side of sandwich. Cook for 2–3 minutes, or until golden. Turn over and cook for another 2–3 minutes. Move the sandwiches to one side of the hotplate to keep warm while cooking the eggs.

Drizzle the light olive oil over the hotplate to lightly grease. Fry the eggs until the whites are just set. Serve a fried egg on each of the toasted sandwiches and drizzle over some extra virgin olive oil to serve.

INGREDIENTS

8 slices Vienna loaf bread, about 15 cm (6 in)
100 g (3½ oz) butter, softened to room temperature
1 tablespoon dijon mustard
4 slices leg ham, each about the size of the slices of bread
200 g (7 oz) gruyère cheese, thinly sliced
1 tablespoon light olive oil
4 eggs
extra virgin olive oil, to serve

PAPRIKA PORK RIBS

Serves 4

Ribs differ from country to country. Americans know ribs as long bones joined with little meat. Ribs can also be cut across the bones with a thick layer of meat left on. This style of rib is popular cut with the Brits where it is sometimes referred to as Jacob's ladder. Aussie ribs are cut in shorter lengths and have the belly and sometimes the skin of the pork still intact.

METHOD

Put the ribs in a large saucepan. Cover with cold water and bring to the boil. Reduce the heat and simmer for 45 minutes. Drain well and put the ribs into a flat dish. Combine the sherry, paprika, cumin, oregano and garlic in a bowl and pour over the ribs. Toss the ribs around so they are well coated in the marinade. Cover and refrigerate overnight.

Remove the ribs from the fridge 1 hour before cooking.

Preheat the barbecue hotplate to medium and drizzle with a little olive oil to lightly grease. Drain the marinade off the ribs, add the 2 tablespoons of olive oil, and reserve. Put the ribs on the hotplate and cook for 5 minutes before turning and cooking for another 5 minutes. Start to brush the reserved marinade over the ribs. Turn and cook for about 3–4 minutes. Repeat brushing and turning for 15–20 minutes until the ribs are dark and the meat tender. You may need to adjust the heat; turning it down if the ribs start to catch and burn. Serve with the lemon wedges on the side.

INGREDIENTS

1.25 kg (2 lb 12 oz) pork spare ribs
125 ml (4 fl oz/½ cup) Spanish
  sherry vinegar
2 tablespoons smoked paprika
3 teaspoons ground cumin
2 teaspoons dried oregano
4 garlic cloves, crushed
2 tablespoons olive oil, plus
  extra, for cooking
lemon wedges, to serve

ROAST SIRLOIN WITH ROOT VEGGIES AND GARLIC CRÈME

Serves 4–6

This is a great cool weather option. In summer, try serving the beef cold, cooked rare, thinly sliced and served with heirloom tomatoes, baby rocket and some olives.

INGREDIENTS

1 teaspoon sea salt
2 teaspoons dried Greek oregano
2 teaspoons ras-el-hanout
   (Moroccan spice blend)
3 tablespoons olive oil
1 sirloin roast, about 1.25 kg
   (2 lb 12 oz)
1 medium sweet potato, cut into
   sticks 10 x 1 cm (4 x ½ in)
2 red onions, skin left on, halved
2 parsnips, peeled and halved
freshly ground black pepper,
   to serve

GARLIC CRÈME

1 garlic bulb
1 tablespoon dijon mustard
½ teaspoon sea salt
¼ teaspoon ground white pepper
3 egg yolks
250 ml (9 fl oz/1 cup) rice bran oil

METHOD

Combine the salt, oregano, half the ras-el-hanout and half the olive oil in a non-metallic bowl and rub over the meat. Set aside at room temperature for 2–3 hours, or cover and refrigerate overnight.

Remove the meat from the fridge 2 hours before cooking. Preheat the barbecue hotplate to medium. To make the garlic crème, loosely wrap the garlic in foil. Sit the garlic on the hotplate, close the lid and cook for 15–20 minutes, until softened and aromatic. Remove and cool, then cut the whole bulb in half crossways and squeeze the flesh out. Put the flesh into a food processor with the mustard, salt, pepper and egg yolks. Process to combine, then very slowly start to add the oil. With the food processor running, pour the rice bran oil in a steady stream until the mixture resembles thick custard. Put into a bowl and set aside.

Increase the barbecue hotplate to high and grill to medium. Put the fat side of the sirloin on the hotplate and cook for 10 minutes. Cook the sirloin for 3 minutes on all sides, until well browned. Reduce the heat to medium. Sit the meat in a 'V'-shaped barbecue rack and sit the rack on the hotplate.

Put the vegetables in a bowl with the remaining olive oil, ras-el-hanout and extra sea salt. Toss to evenly coat in the spice and salt mixture. Strew the veggies over the grill. Close the lid and cook for 15–20 minutes, turning once, until they are golden and tender.

Remove the meat, cover loosely with foil and allow to rest for 15–20 minutes. Carve and serve with the vegetables and spoon over the garlic crème.

ROAST PORK LOIN WITH APPLES

Serves 4

This recipe is a bit festive but can work all year round. It's great to get the big cuts of meat out of the kitchen at Christmas, leaving it free for the rest of the culinary preparations.

METHOD

Make several diagonal incisions in the skin of the pork, cutting through to the flesh.

Put the sea salt, fennel seeds and caraway seeds in a mortar and pound with a pestle until the seeds are crushed. Rub the mixture into the cuts in the pork and set aside at room temperature for 1 hour.

Preheat the barbecue hotplate to high and close the lid to create a hot-oven effect.

Sit the pork on a 'V'-shaped barbecue rack. Sit the rack on the hotplate, close the lid and cook for 30 minutes, until the skin is starting to crisp up around the edges.

Arrange the apples around the pork. Turn the heat down to medium–low and cook for 1 hour. Remove the apples.

For a really crispy skin, increase the heat to high, close the lid and cook the pork for another 10–15 minutes, or until the skin is crisp and golden.

Allow the pork to rest for 15–20 minutes before carving and serving with the apples.

INGREDIENTS

800 g–1 kg (1 lb 12 oz–2 lb 4 oz) pork loin, skin on
2 teaspoons sea salt
1 teaspoon fennel seeds
1 teaspoon caraway seeds
4 green apples

MARRAKESH CHOPS

Serves 6

Truth be known, the inspiration for this recipe comes from a snack I had at a market place in Marrakesh. The snack involved the cheek off a head of lamb and a cumin and salt concoction. The heads were slow cooked, whole, and the cheek meat just fell off the bone. Putting this image to one side, it was very delicious. There is no lamb head here, just some very tasty, and slightly more accessible, lamb loin chops.

CUMIN SALT
1 teaspoon sea salt
1 teaspoon ground cumin

12 thick lamb loin chops
3 tablespoons white wine
3 tablespoons lemon juice
½ teaspoon dried oregano
olive oil, for cooking
lemon wedges, to serve

METHOD

To make the cumin salt, combine the salt and cumin in a small frying pan. Cook over high heat, shaking the pan, until the mixture starts to smoke and is aromatic. Tip into a bowl and cool. Grind to a fine powder in a spice mill or use a mortar and pestle. Set aside until needed.

Put the lamb in a large dish with the wine, lemon juice and oregano, turning to coat in the marinade. Cover and refrigerate for 3 hours or overnight, turning the chops every now and then.

Remove the lamb from the fridge 1 hour before cooking.

Preheat the barbecue hotplate to high. Drizzle a little olive oil on the hotplate to lightly grease. When smoking hot, cook the lamb for 5 minutes. Turn over and cook for a further 3 minutes.

Put the cooked chops on a serving plate and quickly sprinkle the cumin salt all over. Cover loosely with foil and rest for 5–10 minutes.

Serve with the lemon wedges.

RACK OF LAMB WITH MUSTARD AND ROSEMARY CRUST

Serves 4

This is a bit retro, but lovely nonetheless. Normally breadcrumbs would be included, but I find that they dry out too much on the barbie. I would serve this with a simple green salad and some potatoes.

METHOD

Preheat the barbecue hotplate and grill to high and close the lid to create a hot-oven effect.

Combine the mustard, rosemary, garlic and sea salt in a small bowl. Rub the mixture all over the top of the lamb racks.

Sit the lamb rack on a baking rack set over a baking tray half filled with water and sit the dish on the hotplate, close the lid and cook for 20 minutes, or until the mustard crust looks dry, not burnt.

Remove the racks, loosely cover with foil and rest for 10 minutes before carving.

INGREDIENTS

4 tablespoons dijon mustard
2 tablespoons finely chopped
   young rosemary
1 garlic clove, crushed
1 teaspoon sea salt
3 racks of lamb, each with 4 cutlets

LAMB KEBABS WITH SPICED YOGHURT

Serves 3

Lamb meat is made for barbecuing. But keep in mind the lamb leg, like rump in beef, is made up of several different muscles so it will vary in texture and tenderness.

INGREDIENTS

1 small boned leg of lamb, about
    1.25 kg (2 lb 12 oz)
3 tablespoons plain yoghurt
1 teaspoon ground cumin
1 teaspoon ground turmeric
½ teaspoon garam masala
2 teaspoons sea salt
1 white onion, chopped
2 garlic cloves, chopped
1 tablespoon finely grated ginger
1 large handful chopped coriander
    (cilantro) leaves
olive oil, for brushing
lemon wedges, to serve

METHOD

Cut the lamb into large chunks, about 4 cm (1½ in) long. Put the chunks into a large non-metallic bowl.

Put all the other ingredients, except the olive oil and lemon wedges, in a food proceesor and process to make a finely chopped paste. Spoon over the lamb and toss the lamb pieces so they are evenly coated in the marinade.

Cover and set aside at room temperature for 2–4 hours.

Preheat the barbecue grill to medium. Skewer pieces of lamb onto 6 long metal skewers and brush with the olive oil. Cook on the grill for 10 minutes, turning every 2 minutes. Serve with the lemon wedges and a tomato salad, if desired.

BEEF RISSOLES WITH HARISSA

Serves 4

Harissa is a Moroccan chilli-based condiment and takes on many guises. Large dried red chillies can be used, after being soaked and softened in hot water. I make harissa using roasted large fresh red chillies. Harissa would usually include cumin, ground or whole. You could add ground coriander, mint or caraway. Make a big batch of the stuff and stir through mayonnaise, tagines and stews, or just enjoy its unadulterated chilli goodness spread on sandwiches. Or with eggs for breakfast.

METHOD

To make the harissa, preheat the barbecue grill to high. Put the chillies onto the grill and cook for 4–5 minutes, turning often so the chillies are slightly charred and softened.

Set the chillies aside. When cool enough to handle, pull off the stem and put the chillies, including the seeds, into a food processor. Add the garlic, mint and caraway seeds and process, scraping the sides of the bowl, until finely chopped. Add the olive oil to make a chunky paste. Transfer to an airtight container and refrigerate until needed. This will keep for a couple of weeks in the fridge.

To make the rissoles, combine the beef, onion, cumin and parsley in a bowl. Season with sea salt and freshly ground black pepper. Using your hands mix together to make a paste. Refrigerate for 2–3 hours or longer, for flavours to develop.

With wet hands, form the mince into balls that are the size of a golf ball, then flatten to make discs or patties. These can be kept in the fridge for up to a day.

To cook the rissoles, preheat the barbecue hotplate to high. Drizzle the olive oil over the hotplate to grease and cook the rissoles for 3–4 minutes each side.

Serve the rissoles with the rocket, lemon wedges, harissa and chargrilled pitta bread, if desired.

HARISSA

500 g (1 lb 2 oz) large fresh red chillies
2 garlic cloves, chopped
½ teaspoon dried mint
½ teaspoon caraway seeds
250 ml (9 fl oz/1 cup) light olive oil

500 g (1 lb 2 oz) minced (ground) beef
1 onion, grated
1 tablespoon ground cumin
3 tablespoons finely chopped curly parsley
light olive oil, for cooking
rocket (arugula) and lemon wedges, to serve

SMOKY PORK KEBABS

Serves 4

The pork here is kept quite thick and chunky, larger than you would expect skewered meat to be. But the idea is to slide the tasty and tender medallions of pork off the skewer onto your plate. The paprika gives the pork a great colour and a really smoky aroma.

METHOD

Put the pork in a non-metallic bowl or dish. Combine the paprikas, garlic, sherry and oregano in a small bowl, stirring to dissolve the paprika. Pour over the pork and toss around to combine well. Cover and refrigerate for 6 hours or overnight.

Remove the pork from the fridge 30 minutes before cooking.

Preheat the barbecue grill or hotplate to high. Thread several bits of pork onto metal skewers. Cook for 8–10 minutes, turning every 2 minutes or so until golden on all sides. Remove from the heat and allow to rest for 5 minutes.

Serve with the soft baguette or Italian bread rolls and salad leaves.

INGREDIENTS

750–800 g (1 lb 10 oz–1 lb 12 oz) pork fillet, cut into 2 cm (¾ in) thick slices
1 teaspooon hot smoked paprika
2 teaspoons sweet smoked paprika
3 garlic cloves, finely chopped
125 ml (4 fl oz/½ cup) fino sherry
½ teaspoon dried oregano
soft baguette or Italian bread rolls, to serve
salad leaves, to serve

ORANGE AND SPICE PORK MEDALLIONS

Serves 4

Grated onion not only adds flavour to meat but also tenderises it. The marinade here is very basic yet tasty—a good one to have up your sleeve. It would also work nicely with chicken thigh fillets or rump steak.

INGREDIENTS

600–700 g (1 lb 5 oz–1 lb 9 oz)
   pork tenderloin
1 white onion
2 teaspoons sea salt
2 tablespoons orange juice
1 tablespoon ground cumin
2 teaspoons paprika
1 tablespoon olive oil
1 orange, cut into 1 cm (½ in) slices
salad leaves, to serve
coriander (cilantro) sprigs, to serve
   (optional)

METHOD

Trim and cut the tenderloin into 1.5 cm (⅝ in) thick slices and put into a non-metallic dish.

Coarsely grate the onion into a bowl and stir through the sea salt. Set aside for 10 minutes. Press the onion into a sieve so the juice drips over the pork. Discard the onion pulp. Add the orange juice, cumin, paprika and olive oil to the pork and stir to combine. Cover and refrigerate for a few hours or overnight, stirring every now and then.

Remove the pork from the fridge 1 hour before cooking.

Preheat the barbecue hotplate to high. Cook the pork for 3 minutes each side. Set aside. Cook the orange slices for 1–2 minutes on each side, or until caramelised. Serve the pork with the orange slices and salad leaves, with the coriander sprigs scattered over, if using.

FRAGRANT BEEF KEFTA

Serves 4

Kefta is a meatball in Morocco. They can be cooked in a tomato-based sauce and baked in a pot, which could be called a tagine. Ras-el-hanout is a blend of spices, and can vary greatly, somewhat like garam masala in Indian cooking.

METHOD

Put the beef, onion, garlic, ginger, cinnamon, ras-el-hanout, salt, coriander and parsley in a large bowl. Use your hands to combine. Pick the mince up and firmly throw it back into the bowl or onto a clean work surface to remove any air and to tenderise the meat. Cover and refrigerate for 2–6 hours.

Using wet hands, divide the mixture in half. Keep dividing in half until you have 16 portions, roughly about the same size. Again, with wet hands, form each portion into a torpedo shape, tapering at each end.

Preheat the barbecue grill to high.

Brush the olive oil over the meat. Put the kefta on the grill, sprinkle over some extra sea salt, and cook for 5 minutes, without turning or moving. This allows the kefta to form a golden crust so they can then be turned without breaking up. Turn over and cook for another 3–4 minutes. Serve with toasted pitta bread, and a tomato, cucumber and onion salad, if desired.

INGREDIENTS

750 g (1 lb 10 oz) minced (ground) beef
1 red onion, finely chopped
2 garlic cloves, crushed
1 teaspoon ground ginger
2 teaspoons ground cinnamon
2 teaspoons ras-el-hanout (Moroccan spice blend)
1 teaspoon sea salt, plus extra, for seasoning
3 tablespoons finely chopped coriander (cilantro) leaves
3 tablespoons finely chopped flat-leaf (Italian) parsley
3 tablespoons olive oil

QUERÈTARO PORK WITH TOMATILLO AND BEER SALSA

Serves 4–6

I have this really old Mexican cookbook that includes a collection of recipes from some of the posh hotels during the seventies. It's fun to look at but generally not much good to cook from. When flicking through one day I stumbled across a recipe for Querètaro pork. Querètaro is a town in Mexico.

INGREDIENTS
750 ml (26 fl oz/3 cups) milk
1 cinnamon stick
1 garlic bulb, cut in half crossways
2 bay leaves
2 thyme sprigs
1 butterflied pork shoulder, skin removed
light olive oil, for cooking
tortillas, to serve (optional)

TOMATILLO AND BEER SALSA
400 g (14 oz/2 cups) drained tinned tomatillos
125 ml (4 fl oz/½ cup) Mexican beer
2 large green chillies, chopped
1 very large handful coriander (cilantro) leaves

METHOD
Combine the milk, cinnamon stick, garlic, bay leaves and thyme sprigs in a saucepan. Cook on low heat for 3–4 minutes, without letting it boil. Remove from the heat and leave to cool to room temperature, allowing the flavours to infuse.

Put the pork in a large bowl and pour over the milk. Cover and refrigerate for 24 hours, turning the pork every now and then.

To make the salsa, put all the ingredients in a food processor and blend to make a chunky paste. Put into a bowl and set aside.

Remove the pork from the fridge 2 hours before cooking.

Preheat the barbecue hotplate to high and drizzle with some olive oil to lightly grease.

Drain the pork well and pat dry. Sear each side of the pork on the hotplate until well browned. Turn the heat down to low and sit the pork on a 'V'-shaped barbecue rack set over a baking tray half filled with water. Close the barbecue lid and cook, topping up the water as it evaporates, for 1½ hours or until the pork is very tender.

Roughly shred the pork with two forks or a knife and serve with the tomatillo and beer salsa and tortillas, if desired.

THE SEA

I'VE BEEN LUCKY ENOUGH TO HAVE WORK THAT HAS ALLOWED me to travel all over the place. From Portland, Maine to Portland, Oregon. Dublin to Marrakesh. Sydney's Chinatown to Chinatown, New York City. And with seafood, I find myself looking towards several cuisines for flavour inspiration. The heady spices of the Middle East and North Africa. Warming Spanish paprika. Zesty lemon and lime from Southeast Asia, with palate-refreshing herbs to match—lemongrass, coriander and mint.

Of course, it is tricky trying to cook some varieties of seafood on the barbecue. So I find myself turning towards a stock standard few: raw prawns—pretty much of all sizes, whole fish and fish fillets, cuttlefish, squid, lobster tails and octopus. These creatures can be marinated and cooked quickly and with ease.

And when barbecuing seafood I use a few tricks. Put a sheet of baking paper on the hotplate when cooking tender fish fillets or large whole fish. The paper will prevent the delicate skin of the fish from sticking and make it much easier to turn over and remove from the hotplate. Fish wrapped in parcels of baking paper or cooking foil gently steam the delicate flesh and impart the flavours of the marinade and seasonings. Skewers are ideal for cooking smaller pieces of seafood—scallops, cubes of fish fillet or smaller prawns. Season all seafood well with sea salt. A little extra salt on fish skin will help it cook to a crisp on the hotplate.

Barbecuing seafood is all too easy. And so it should be.

A BIG SICILIAN FLAVOURED FISH

Serves 6

Wonderful flavours and cooking method here, something I stumbled across by accident. I bought a rather large 'V'-shaped barbecue rack, which did not fit on my barbecue, unless it was inverted to be an upside down 'V'. Perfect for a whole fish to sit on and cook to perfection. I am a big fan of the fennel seed and chilli flake combo but if you find these too spicy or intense don't let that stop you from experiencing cooking fish this way.

INGREDIENTS

1 big snapper, about 2 kg
   (4 lb 8 oz), cleaned, gutted
   and scaled
1 teaspoon chilli flakes
1 teaspoon fennel seeds
2 garlic cloves, chopped
1 teaspoon sea salt
3 tablespoons olive oil
2 tablespoons finely chopped
   flat-leaf (Italian) parsley
   (optional), to serve
lemon cheeks, to serve

METHOD

Give the fish a good wash and dry with paper towel. Make several, deep diagonal cuts across each side of the fish. Scrunch up some baking paper and run under cold water. Shake out any excess water and put the scrunched paper inside the cavity of the fish.

Combine the chilli flakes, fennel seeds, garlic, sea salt and olive oil in a small bowl. Brush all over the fish and into the cuts.

Preheat the barbecue hotplate and grill to high and close the lid to create a hot-oven effect. Turn a 'V'-shaped barbecue rack upside down. Sit the fish on the inverted V of the rack so it is upright.

Sit the rack on the hotplate, close the lid and cook for 20–25 minutes, until the flesh of the fish is white and easily pulls away from the bones.

Transfer to a serving plate. Sprinkle with the parsley, if using, and serve with the lemon cheeks.

EXOTIC SPICED CUTTLEFISH

Serves 4

Fresh cuttlefish is a gem to cook with. Many fresh seafood outlets may even clean it for you. I find it more tender than squid and its rather unattractive looks scare people off, which means it costs less.

METHOD

Put the salt and spices in a small frying pan and cook over high heat, shaking the pan, until the spices begin to smoke. Remove from the heat, tip into a bowl and set aside.

Use a sharp knife to scrape any bits of dark skin off the cuttlefish. Cut open the hood of the cuttlefish and use a small knife to scrape it clean. Slice the cuttlefish into strips, no wider than 1 cm (½ in). Put into a bowl with the olive oil, tossing to coat the cuttlefish.

Preheat the barbecue hotplate to high.

Put the cuttlefish on the hotplate, using tongs to spread out. Cook for just a minute or two, until white and curled up. Turn over and cook for another minute. Put the cuttlefish in a bowl and sprinkle over the spice mixture, shaking the bowl to coat.

Serve with the lemon wedges, if using.

INGREDIENTS

1 teaspoon sea salt
½ teaspoon ground coriander
½ teaspoon ground cumin
½ teaspoon smoked paprika
½ teaspoon ras-el-hanout
   (Moroccan spice blend)
750 g (1 lb 10 oz) cuttlefish
   hoods, cleaned
1 tablespoon olive oil
lemon wedges, to serve (optional)

PRAWN AND CHORIZO SKEWERS

Serves 4

Chonza is the nickname I have for the chorizo we use, actually called 'cheeky chorizo' because of the extra chilli used in it. Raw chorizo is used here so it has to be cooked before eating. Chorizo should be a deep and rich colour and jam-packed with garlic and paprika. Please don't use the chorizo that looks like cabanossi.

INGREDIENTS

3 raw chorizo, about 350 g (12 oz)
16 raw large prawns (shrimp), peeled and deveined, leaving the tails intact
2 tablespoons olive oil
2 tablespoons lemon juice
½ teaspoon good quality dried mint
lemon cheeks, to serve

METHOD

Cut the chorizo into 16 chunks similar in thickness to the prawns. Put the chorizo in a bowl with the prawns, olive oil, lemon juice and mint. Toss the ingredients around to combine. Set aside at room temperature for 30 minutes or cover and refrigerate for 3–6 hours.

Remove from the fridge 30 minutes before cooking.

Preheat the barbecue grill or hotplate to high.

Put 2 pieces of chorizo and 2 prawns on each of the 8 skewers. Cook the skewers for 3–4 minutes on each side, or until cooked through.

Serve with the lemon cheeks and barbecued truss cherry tomatoes, if desired.

SEAFOOD LEMONGRASS SKEWERS

Serves 6

This recipe has Vietnam written all over it. Simple, fresh flavours, with lemongrass of course. I have an indelible memory of lemongrass, which I use here as a skewer. Tinned sugarcane, split or cut into thinner pieces, is also an effective and exotic skewer.

METHOD

Put the chilli, garlic, spring onion, turmeric, ground coriander, shrimp paste, tamarind purée, lime leaves, lemongrass, rice bran oil, coconut cream and brown sugar in a food processor. Process until finely chopped and scrape the mixture into a bowl.

Put the prawn meat and fish in the food processor and process to a mince. Scrape into the bowl with the spice mix and stir well to combine.

Using wet hands, take a generous 3 tablespoons of the mixture and form into a log around a length of lemongrass. Repeat with the remaining mixture.

Preheat the barbecue hotplate to high. Cook the skewers for 5 minutes. Carefully turn over and cook for another 5 minutes. Serve with the coriander sprigs.

INGREDIENTS

5 large red chillies, chopped
4 garlic cloves, chopped
4 spring onions (scallions), chopped
¼ teaspoon ground turmeric
½ teaspoon ground coriander
1 teaspoon shrimp paste
2 tablespoons tamarind purée
2 makrut (kaffir lime) leaves, finely
  shredded
1 tablespoon finely chopped
  lemongrass, white part only
2 tablespoons rice bran oil
3 tablespoons coconut cream
2 tablespoons brown sugar
400 g raw prawn (shrimp) meat
400 g white fish fillet
6 lemongrass stalks, cut in 15 cm
  (6 in) lengths, to make 12
  skewers
coriander (cilantro) sprigs, to serve

TROUT WITH PERSIAN RICE

Serves 4

It is very typical of North African and Middle Eastern cookery to have sweet and aromatic spices used with meat, fish and chicken. There is that amazing Moroccan dish 'bastilla', a pie made of chicken or pigeon meat, cooked in filo and sprinkled with cinnamon and icing sugar. The flavours sound incongruous but it actually works like a treat. Like using cinnamon with fish; who would have thought?

PERSIAN RICE

2 tablespoons butter
1 small red onion, thinly sliced
2 teaspoons finely grated ginger
2 teaspoons ground cinnamon
2 tablespoons slivered almonds, roughly chopped
110 g (3¾ oz/½ cup) short-grain rice
2 tablespoons finely chopped coriander (cilantro) leaves
2 tablespoons finely chopped mint
2 tablespoons finely chopped flat-leaf (Italian) parsley

4 small rainbow trout, cleaned, gutted and scaled
olive oil, for cooking

METHOD

Heat the butter in a small saucepan over medium heat. When the butter is sizzling, add the onion and cook for 2–3 minutes or until softened. Stir in the ginger and cinnamon and cook for 1 minute or until aromatic. Stir in the almonds and rice. Add enough water to the pan so it just covers the rice and bring to the boil. Reduce the heat and simmer for about 10 minutes, or until most of the liquid has been absorbed by the rice. Quickly fluff with a fork then cover and set aside for 20 minutes. Stir through the herbs and season to taste.

Spoon the rice mixture into the trout cavity.

Preheat the barbecue hotplate to medium. Lay a sheet of baking paper on the hotplate and brush the paper with the olive oil. Lay the trout on the paper, close the lid and cook for 10 minutes. Carefully turn the trout over and cook for another 8–10 minutes, or until just cooked through.

OLD-SCHOOL GARLIC PRAWNS

Serves 4

In saying old-school I mean retro. And what a novel dish this was—molten hot oil, bubbling in cast-iron pots with a few prawns and some garlic thrown in. It probably wasn't the safest thing to eat but fun all the same. And how tasty was it to mop up the garlicky oil with some bread?

METHOD

Preheat the barbecue hotplate to high.

Divide the oil between four small cast-iron garlic prawn pots, or small stainless steel cooking bowls. Put the pots on the hotplate, close the lid and leave for 10 minutes until the oil heats up.

The oil is ready when the surface is shimmering. Use large metal tongs to put 6 prawns in each pot. Close the lid and cook for 3–4 minutes, or until the prawns are pink. Divide the garlic, salt, almonds and parsley into four even-sized portions and stir a portion into each of the pots. Carefully transfer the pots to heatproof plates. Serve with the crusty bread for dipping.

INGREDIENTS

250 ml (9 fl oz/1 cup) olive oil

24 raw large prawns (shrimp), peeled and deveined, leaving the tails intact

8 garlic cloves, finely chopped

1 teaspoon sea salt

2 tablespoons roughly chopped flaked almonds

2 tablespoons finely chopped curly parsley

crusty bread, to serve

FIVE-SPICE FISH PARCELS

Serves 4

Okay, so there are only four spices here. Sichuan pepper would also be included in any traditional five-spice mixture, which is endemic to Chinese cookery. Although, there is a Bengali five-spice combination called panch phora—but that's another thing altogether.

SAUCE
8 star anise
4 whole cloves
½ teaspoon fennel seeds
4 small cinnamon sticks
3 tablespoons light soy sauce
1 tablespoon shaved palm sugar
   (jaggery) or dark brown sugar
1 tablespoon finely grated ginger

4 x 200 g (7 oz) blue eye, or a firm
   white-fleshed fish, fillets

METHOD
Combine all the sauce ingredients in a small saucepan. Bring to the boil over high heat, stirring to dissolve the sugar. Reduce the heat and simmer for 2–3 minutes. Pour into a bowl and set aside to cool.

Add the fish to the sauce mixture, tossing to coat all over. Cover and refrigerate for up to 3 hours.

Remove the fish from the fridge 30 minutes before cooking.

Tear off four sheets of baking paper large enough to wrap a piece of the fish entirely. Wet the paper, then shake off any excess water.

Sit a piece of fish in the centre of each piece of paper. Spoon over the sauce ensuring you have 2 star anise, 1 whole clove and 1 cinnamon stick on each. Wrap the fish in the paper to firmly enclose.

Preheat the barbecue grill to high. Sit the parcels on the grill, close the lid and cook for 8–10 minutes. Serve with Asian greens, if desired.

WHOLE FISH WITH JALAPEÑO CHILLIES, LEMON AND HERBS

Serves 4

Cooking fish in foil or baking paper is not novel. One of the most simple yet tasty recipes is to wrap fish fillets in baking paper with nothing more than lemon slices, dill and butter. This recipe has more of a punch with the inclusion of jalapeños.

METHOD

Preheat the barbecue grill or hotplate to high.

Rinse the fish with cold water and pat dry with a paper towel. Tear off four large pieces of foil and place four slightly smaller pieces of baking paper on top and put a fish on each.

Put some lemon slices inside the cavity of each fish. Put about 1 tablespoon of butter on top of each fish, top with the herbs and chilli and pour over the lemon juice. Season well with sea salt and freshly ground black pepper. Loosely wrap the fish in the foil and sit on the barbecue. Close the lid and cook for 8–10 minutes. Allow to sit in the foil for 10 minutes before opening the parcels to serve.

INGREDIENTS

4 small whole white-fleshed fish, such as snapper, about 400 g (14 oz) each, cleaned, gutted and scaled

1 lemon, thinly sliced

100 g (3½ oz) unsalted butter, diced

2 tablespoons roughly chopped dill

1 tablespoon finely chopped flat-leaf (Italian) parsley

2 tablespoons finely chopped jalapeño chillies, in brine, drained

3 tablespoons lemon juice

SWORDFISH KEBABS

Serves 4

Swordfish to me is about the texture of the meat. And this is a meaty fish. Like tuna, it lends itself to being cooked as you would a steak and when cubed and skewered it doesn't fall apart like soft-textured fish.

INGREDIENTS
750 g (1 lb 10 oz) swordfish steaks,
    skin removed and cut into
    3–4 cm (1¼–1½ in) pieces
3 tablespoons olive oil
4 garlic cloves, finely chopped
3 tablespoons finely chopped
    flat-leaf (Italian) parsley
3 tablespoons lemon juice
4 roma (plum) tomatoes, quartered
2 red onions, peeled and each cut
    into 8 wedges
1 green capsicum (pepper), cut into
    2–3 cm (¾–1¼ in) pieces
chargrilled lemon cheeks, to serve

METHOD
Put the swordfish in a bowl with the olive oil, garlic, parsley and lemon juice. Set aside at room temperature for 30 minutes.

Preheat the barbecue hotplate to high. Thread pieces of fish, tomato, onion wedges and green capsicum onto 8 long metal skewers. Reserve the marinade.

Cook the skewers for about 8 minutes, basting with the reserved marinade, turning every 2 minutes, until the fish is cooked through.

Serve with the chargrilled lemon cheeks.

RAS-EL-HANOUT SPICED SWORDFISH

Serves 4

In the Derb, or market laneways in Marrakesh, each spice shop will have its own ras-el-hanout, or 'top shelf' spice blend. A bit like the Indian spice blend garam masala, each version will be different from the next.

SPICE MIX
1 teaspoon sea salt
1 teaspoon smoked paprika
1 teaspoon ras-el-hanout
   (Moroccan spice blend)

750 g (1 lb 10 oz) swordfish,
   cleaned, gutted and scaled,
   cut into large chunks
2 tablespoons olive oil
lemon wedges, to serve

METHOD
To make the spice mix, put the spices in a small frying pan. Cook on high heat, shaking the pan, until the spices just start to smoke but do not burn. Tip the spices into a bowl and set aside.

Put the swordfish into a bowl with the olive oil and toss to coat.

Preheat the barbecue hotplate to high.

Tumble the fish pieces over the hotplate and cook for 6–8 minutes, turning every couple of minutes until the fish is golden and cooked through. Put the fish in a bowl. Add the spice mix to the fish, shaking the bowl so the fish is coated in the spices. Serve with the lemon wedges.

VIETNAMESE RICE PAPER ROLLS WITH BLUE EYE, CASHEW AND CORIANDER

Serves 4

Rice paper rolls are a unique eating experience. They can be filled with pork, chicken and prawns, fragrant herbs and even noodles. The rice paper is softened in water and is ready to eat. But they can actually be pan-fried or barbecued, which is what you need to do here to cook the enclosed raw fish.

METHOD

To make the coriander and cashew paste, put all the ingredients in a food processor and process until the mixture looks like a chunky pesto. Put the mixture into a bowl and refrigerate. The paste can be made a day before.

Cut the fish into 8 evenly sized pieces. Add the fish to the prepared paste and rub the paste all over the fish. Set aside.

Lay a clean tea towel (dish towel) on a work surface. Put warm water into a bowl. One at a time, soak each rice paper for 2–3 minutes so they really soften. Lay the rice papers flat on the tea towel.

Sit a piece of fish in the centre of each rice paper. Spoon any excess paste over each fish. Fold the sides over then roll up to firmly enclose the fish.

Preheat the barbecue hotplate to high. Lightly brush with olive oil to grease. Sit the rice paper rolls on the hotplate, close the lid and cook for 5 minutes. Try to avoid turning the rolls before this time. They need to develop a golden crust so they do not tear. Use a metal spatula to slide underneath each roll and turn it over. Cook, covered, for another 5 minutes.

Serve with the lettuce leaves and lime wedges.

CORIANDER AND CASHEW PASTE

1 small bunch coriander (cilantro)
50 g (1¾ oz) cashews, roasted
1 tablespoon finely grated ginger
1 teaspoon sugar
2 tablespoons fish sauce
¼ teaspoon ground white pepper
2 teaspoons light olive oil

500 g (1 lb 2 oz) blue eye, or a firm
    white-fleshed fish, fillets
8 small Vietnamese rice papers
olive oil, for cooking
butter lettuce leaves, to serve
lime wedges, to serve

CRISPY SALT AND CHILLI SALMON

Serves 4

The trick to the perfect barbecued fish is making sure your hotplate is really hot before adding the fish. And not moving the fish before the end of the cooking time as the skin will tear. If you allow the skin to contract with the heat of the hotplate, turning it will be easy.

METHOD

Finely grind the peppercorns, chilli flakes and sea salt using a spice mill or mortar and pestle. Set aside.

Wash the salmon fillets and pat dry with a paper towel. Refrigerate the salmon, uncovered, skin side up, for 3 hours or overnight.

Remove the salmon from the fridge30 minutes before cooking. Sprinkle the salt mixture evenly over the skin.

Heat the barbecue hotplate to high and lightly grease with olive oil.

Lay the salmon, skin side down, on the hotplate. Cook without moving for 5 minutes until a very crisp, golden skin forms. Use a metal spatula to flip the fish over and cook for another 2 minutes. Serve with the lime wedges on the side.

INGREDIENTS

½ teaspoon sichuan peppercorns
½ teaspoon chilli flakes
½ teaspoon sea salt
4 salmon fillets, about 180–200 g
(6–7 oz) each, skin on
olive oil, for cooking
lime wedges, to serve

SALT AND PEPPER CALAMARI

Serves 4

Salt and pepper calamari could well be the most ubiquitous item on Asian menus. I would say that most restaurant versions would be deep-fried. Cooking the calamari on a very hot hotplate will give you a good result. Try this with prawns, cooking for just a minute or two on each side until pink and curled, and tossing to coat in the salt and pepper mix.

INGREDIENTS

750 g (1 lb 10 oz) calamari tubes, cleaned
2 tablespoons light olive oil
2 large red chillies, finely chopped
2 garlic cloves, finely chopped
1 teaspoon sea salt flakes
1 teaspoon white peppercorns
1 teaspoon sichuan peppercorns
coriander (cilantro) leaves, chopped, to serve
lemon cheeks, to serve

METHOD

Slice the calamari into 1 cm (½ in) strips and put into a bowl with the olive oil, chilli and garlic, tossing the calamari to coat in the mixture. Refrigerate until needed.

Put the sea salt flakes and peppercorns in a small frying pan and cook over high heat until smoking hot. Shake the pan a few times then tip the mix into a bowl to cool. When cool, use a spice grinder or mortar and pestle to grind the spices to a coarse powder.

Preheat the barbecue hotplate to high. Put the calamari onto the hotplate, moving around with tongs so the strips are spread apart. Cook for 2 minutes then start to turn the calamari over. Cook for another 2 minutes, then put the calamari into a large bowl. Add the pepper spice and toss to coat the calamari in the spices. Sprinkle with the chopped coriander and serve with the lemon cheeks.

THAI PEPPER GARLIC PRAWNS

Serves 4

The flavour combo of coriander, garlic and fish sauce is very Thai—using all the coriander, from roots to crown. This could be used with whole fish or chicken drumsticks. Cutting deep slashes into the thicker parts of the fish or chicken drumstick will ensure more even cooking. The trick to a well-cooked prawn is not to cook it until it's well done. As soon as the prawn has changed colour and is curled up it is ready.

METHOD

Cut about 3–4 cm (1¼–1½ in) from the root end of the coriander. Rinse the roots, then finely chop and put into a mortar. Roughly chop the coriander leaves and set aside.

Add the garlic and peppercorns to the coriander roots and, using a pestle, pound to a paste. Tip the paste into a bowl. Stir in the brown sugar and fish sauce. Add the prawns and toss to coat with the paste. Set aside at room temperature for 30 minutes or cover and refrigerate for 3–6 hours.

Remove the prawns from the fridge 30 minutes before cooking.

Heat the barbecue hotplate to high. Drizzle the vegetable oil over the hotplate to grease. Add the prawns and cook for 2 minutes each side, until pink, curled up and aromatic. Serve with the reserved chopped coriander leaves sprinkled over and the lime wedges on the side.

INGREDIENTS

1 bunch coriander (cilantro)
4 garlic cloves, chopped
1 tablespoon white peppercorns
2 tablespoons brown sugar
2 tablespoons fish sauce
16 raw large prawns (shrimp), peeled and deveined, leaving the tails intact
vegetable oil, for cooking
lime wedges, to serve

BARBECUED SNAPPER WITH MEXICAN SALSA

Serves 6

The same smoky flavour you get when cooking eggplant for baba ghanoush can be achieved with any other soft veggies, such as tomatoes, garlic and shallots. If you decide to go down the Thai flavour path, these veggies would be peeled and processed with some fish sauce and sugar. Or you could take a completely different turn and add some Mexican flavours, like fiery chipotle and coriander. This is a very flavoursome base for a sauce to use with barbecued fish or chicken.

MEXICAN SALSA

2 tomatoes
4 garlic cloves, unpeeled
1 onion, skin left on and halved
3 tablespoons orange juice
2 tablespoons red wine vinegar
1 tablespoon chipotle chilli powder
2 tablespoons brown sugar
3 tablespoons chopped coriander
    (cilantro) leaves

1 large snapper, about 2 kg
    (4 lb 8 oz), cleaned, gutted
    and scaled
2 tablespoons olive oil, plus extra,
    for cooking
2 teaspoons sea salt
coriander (cilantro), roughly
    chopped, to serve
lime wedges, to serve

METHOD

Preheat the barbecue grill to high.

To make the Mexican salsa, put the tomatoes, garlic and onion on the grill, turning constantly and removing from the grill when the skin of each is charred and blistered. Allow to cool.

Peel the vegetables, roughly chop and put into a food processor with the orange juice, vinegar, chipotle chilli powder, brown sugar and coriander. Process to a smooth paste.

Make several deep, diagonal cuts across each side of the fish. Combine the olive oil and sea salt in a bowl and rub all over the fish.

Preheat the barbecue hotplate to medium and close the lid to create a hot-oven effect.

Brush a large sheet of baking paper with a little olive oil. Lay the fish on the baking paper and spread 1 tablespoon of the salsa onto each side of the fish and put onto the hotplate. Close the lid and cook for 15 minutes. Carefully turn the fish over and cook, covered, for 10 minutes.

Slide the fish onto a serving platter. Spoon over the remaining salsa, sprinkle with the coriander and serve with the lime wedges.

LOBSTER TAILS WITH CHILLI AND GARLIC BUTTER

Serves 4

Lobsters are odd creatures. But then again, so are prawns, which I personally prefer. There is something about the expense of lobster that puts pressure on the cook to do something really fancy with it. This is where mistakes are made. Keep it simple. No béchamel or white sauce, no cheese and no flambé. Cook the lobster simply and quickly, basted with some lovely, fresh flavours. That's all you need do.

METHOD

Combine the butter, chilli flakes, garlic and parsley in a small bowl. Season with a little sea salt and set aside.

Cut the lobster tails in half lengthways and spread the butter mixture over the cut sides.

Preheat the barbecue hotplate to medium. Lay the lobster, shell side down, on the hotplate, close the lid and cook for 10 minutes, or until the lobster meat is white and cooked through. Serve with the lemon cheeks.

INGREDIENTS

75 g (2½ oz) unsalted butter, softened to room temperature
½ teaspoon chilli flakes
2 garlic cloves, crushed
1 tablespoon finely chopped flat-leaf (Italian) parsley
2 lobster tails, about 320 g (11¼ oz) each
lemon cheeks, to serve

PRAWNS WITH GARLIC AND VINEGAR

Serves 4

Pouring hot oil on garlic (or on any combination of garlic, ginger and spring onion, for that matter) is very Cantonese. It is also, as I recently discovered, a technique used in Iberian cooking. The hot oil softens the garlic, making it more palatable, at the same time as infusing the oil with the flavour of the garlic.

INGREDIENTS

8 garlic cloves, finely chopped
3 tablespoons light olive oil
3 tablespoons white wine vinegar
1 tablespoon Spanish sweet
    paprika
1 teaspoon sea salt
24 raw large prawns (shrimp),
    peeled and deveined, leaving
    the tails intact
baby rocket leaves, to serve
lemon wedges, to serve (optional)

METHOD

Put the garlic in a small heatproof bowl. Put the olive oil in a small saucepan and heat over high heat until hot. Pour the oil over the garlic, allowing it to sizzle for just a few seconds then quickly add the vinegar, paprika and sea salt. Stir to combine and set aside until cool.

Put the prawns in a large bowl. Pour over the garlic mixture, stirring well so the prawns are coated in the sauce. Set aside at room temperature for 30 minutes or cover and refrigerate for 3–6 hours.

Remove the prawns from the fridge 30 minutes before cooking.

Preheat the barbecue hotplate to high.

Spread the prawns over the hotplate so they don't overlap. You may have to cook them in a couple of batches. Cook for 3 minutes, turn over and cook for another 2 minutes, until pink, curled up and cooked through.

Scatter over the rocket and serve with the lemon wedges, if using.

OCEAN TROUT FILLET WITH GINGER AND SHALLOTS

Serves 4

Ocean trout is a terrifically coloured fish. Beautiful to look at and beautiful to eat. Please avoid overcooking this one. Ideally, you want the fish to be a dusty pink on the outside while retaining a glossy orange centre. Despite its robust colour this delicately flavoured fish is complemented by light Asian flavours.

METHOD

Put the fish on a large plate or baking tray. Rub the Chinese rice wine all over the fish and season with sea salt and ground white pepper. Set aside for 30 minutes.

Tear off a large sheet of foil and lay on a work surface. Tear off a similar sized sheet of baking paper and lay on top of the foil.

Sit the fish in the centre, skin side down.

Combine the stock, soy sauce and sugar in a small bowl to dissolve the sugar then pour the mixture over the fish.

Scatter the ginger and the white part of the spring onions over the fish. Loosely wrap the fish in the foil.

Preheat the barbecue hotplate to high and close the lid to create a hot-oven effect.

Lay the fish on the hotplate, close the lid and cook for 10 minutes. Leave the fish wrapped and transfer to a serving platter.

Barbecue the lime cheeks for 1–2 minutes or until caramelised.

Put the oil in a small saucepan and sit the saucepan on the hotplate. When the surface of the oil is shimmering and smoking hot, unwrap the fish and carefully pour the hot oil over the fish.

Scatter the green parts of the spring onion and the coriander on top and sprinkle over some white pepper. Serve with the lime cheeks.

INGREDIENTS

1 ocean trout fillet, about 1 kg (2 lb 4 oz), skin on
1 tablespoon Chinese rice wine
pinch of ground white pepper, plus extra, to serve
3 tablespoons chicken stock
1 tablespoon light soy sauce
1 teaspoon caster (superfine) sugar
5 cm (2 in) piece of ginger, shredded as finely as possible
6 spring onions (scallions), white and green parts thinly sliced on an angle, and kept separate
4 lime cheeks, to serve
3 tablespoons rice bran oil
1 handful chopped coriander (cilantro) leaves and stems, to serve

THE GARDEN

YOU MAY NOT THINK VEGGIES AND BARBIES GO TOGETHER.
But think again. What about potatoes baked whole in their jackets,
topped with sour cream or labneh? Corn on the cob smothered in
butter? Chargrilled eggplant, capsicum and zucchini tossed with
feta cheese and herbs and a garlicky oil? Roasted tomatoes doused
in olive oil, sprinkled with oregano and sea salt? There is a theme to
my barbecued veggies—the flavours of Italy, Asia and the Middle
East dominate, and for good reason. These cultures have a long
and strong history of markets and local produce. Fresh and
flavoursome food.

I have included lots of vine veggies here; eggplant probably wins
hands down for its versatility (and it's my own personal favourite), the
same goes for tomatoes and zucchini. These veggies absorb flavour.
A quick lick of a flame and they are charred and tender, ready to be
doused in vinegar and olive oil and tossed with gutsy seasonings and
fresh herbs. Delish.

Freshness and seasonality is important and a trip to your local
farmers' market is in order. Choose eggplant with tight and shiny
skins. Summer tomatoes should smell like no other and, if you can,
get your hands on some heirloom varieties. Fennel should be
unbruised with feathery tops and herbs plump and proud. It is
tempting to buy dirt-cheap garlic but this often comes from afar and
is sprayed with all sorts of nasty things. Hunt down a local garlic
grower. It may cost more but it will taste great and last for ages.

So let's not try and reinvent the wheel here. Let's do the opposite.
Let the wheel be the wheel, or the eggplant be the eggplant and
the pumpkin be the pumpkin, if you know what I mean. This is the
approach I take when cooking veggies on the barbecue. There is no
finely diced carrot, celery or onion in my book. Well, not in one of my
barbecue books at least. This is all about vegetables in all their raw,
naked glory.

VEGETABLE AND HALOUMI SKEWERS

Serves 4

Haloumi is one of those ingredients that seemed to come from nowhere to become one of my favourite things to cook. Here it is cubed and skewered with eggplant and zucchini. You could also slice the haloumi into 1 cm thick 'steaks', marinate in a mixture of dried chilli flakes, dried oregano, olive oil and lemon juice and cook on the grill until a golden crust is formed.

INGREDIENTS

500 g (1 lb 2 oz) haloumi cheese
2 Japanese eggplants (aubergines)
2 zucchini (courgettes)
2 tablespoons olive oil, plus extra, for cooking
2 tablespoons apple cider vinegar
2 teaspoons cumin seeds
1 teaspoon chilli flakes
2 large handfuls baby rocket (arugula) leaves

METHOD

Soak some bamboo skewers for 30 minutes. Cut the haloumi cheese, eggplant and zucchini into similar sized pieces of about 2 cm (¾ in). Thread two pieces of the cheese alternately with the vegetables onto bamboo skewers and lay the skewers on a flat dish. Mix the olive oil, vinegar, cumin seeds and chilli in a small bowl and pour over the skewers. Set aside at room temperature for a couple of hours.

Preheat the barbecue hotplate to high and drizzle over a little olive oil to lightly grease. Put the skewers on the hotplate, reserving the marinade in the dish, and cook for 2–3 minutes, or until a dark golden crust is formed on the haloumi. Use a spatula to turn the skewers over and cook for another 2 minutes. Put the rocket on a serving plate with the skewers on top. Pour over the reserved marinade.

Serve with couscous, if desired.

INDIAN SPICED EGGPLANT

Serves 4-6

Take note of this method of adding seasoning and flavour to just-cooked eggplant. The heat of the eggplant releases the fragrant oil in the spices. Eggplant is a highly absorbent veggie, you will notice how much oil it sucks up when being fried.

METHOD

Cut the eggplant lengthways into large wedges.

Preheat the barbecue grill to medium. Put the eggplant in a bowl with the rice bran oil and toss to coat in the oil. Tumble the eggplant onto the grill and cook for 12–15 minutes, using tongs to turn often until golden and just tender. Put into a bowl.

Combine the olive oil, garlic, cumin and chilli powder in a small bowl. Add the dressing to the eggplant while it is still hot and toss to coat in the spice mixture.

Smear the labneh onto a serving platter. Spoon the eggplant over and scatter over the mint.

INGREDIENTS

2 medium sized eggplants (aubergines)
2 tablespoons rice bran oil
3 teaspoons salt
2 tablespoons olive oil
1 garlic clove, crushed
1 teaspoon ground cumin
½ teaspoon chilli powder
125 g (4½ oz/½ cup) labneh (strained yoghurt)
1 large handful mint, roughly torn

KAFFIR LIME LEAF AND LEMONGRASS TOFU

Serves 4

I can totally understand if you do not enjoy tofu as it is often cooked really badly. I mean, if you cooked a fillet steak for 20 minutes each side you probably wouldn't like it either. Tofu is about the texture. It is a chameleon of sorts and takes on the flavours it is cooked with. So when cooked well (and by this I generally mean simply and quickly), and used with other flavours, you will understand why tofu is no longer only enjoyed by vegetarians. If you can't get your hands on kecap manis, soy sauce with a little brown sugar will do the job nicely.

INGREDIENTS

2 lemongrass stalks, white part
   only, chopped
2 garlic cloves, chopped
2 makrut (kaffir lime) leaves, thinly
   sliced
1 tablespoon finely grated ginger
2 tablespoons fish sauce
2 tablespoons vegetable oil
1 teaspoon caster (superfine) sugar
300 g (10½ oz) block firm tofu
kecap manis, to serve
coriander (cilantro) sprigs, to serve

METHOD

Put the lemongrass, garlic, lime leaves, ginger, fish sauce, vegetable oil and sugar in a food processor and blend to make a chunky sauce. Transfer to a bowl with the tofu. Gently turn the tofu so it is evenly covered in the mixture. Set aside at room temperature for a couple of hours.

Preheat the barbecue hotplate to medium. Put the block of tofu on the hotplate, scraping any of the sauce over the tofu. Close the lid and cook for 5 minutes. Using a large spatula, turn over the tofu. The lemongrass mixture will have cooked golden and charred in some places. Cook, covered, for another 5 minutes.

Cut into large cubes, transfer to a serving plate, drizzle with the kecap manis and scatter over the coriander.

BARBECUED CORN WITH HOT SALSA

Serves 4

I had a corn recipe in the original *Fired Up*, which proved to be really popular. It involved serving barbecued corn with butter, lime juice and parmesan cheese. Parmesan may sound odd but it adds an extra savoury element—something the Japanese call umami.

METHOD

To make the salsa, combine all the ingredients in a large bowl and set aside.

Preheat the barbecue hotplate to high. Brush the corn with some of the butter and cook for 8–10 minutes, turning and brushing with more butter every couple of minutes, until the corn is starting to char around the edges.

Put the corn into the bowl with the salsa and toss to combine. Season well with salt and freshly ground black pepper. Serve warm sprinkled with the parmesan cheese.

SALSA

2 tablespoons olive oil
1 tablespoon lime juice
3 tablespoons finely diced roasted piquillo pepper or red capsicum (pepper)
3 tablespoons chopped jalapeño chillies, in brine, drained
1 small handful roughly chopped coriander (cilantro) leaves
2 spring onions (scallions), thinly sliced

4 fresh corn cobs
3 tablespoons melted butter
35 g (1¼ oz/¼ cup) finely grated parmesan cheese

BALINESE GRILLED EGGPLANT WITH TOMATO SAMBAL

Serves 4

Sambal is to Bali and Indonesia what harissa is to Morocco. This is an unadulterated chilli sauce—hot, spicy and with a real kick. It is added to curries and used as a condiment in its own right with grilled meats.

SAMBAL
4 ripe tomatoes
4 garlic cloves, unpeeled
2 red Asian shallots
1 teaspoon shrimp paste
1 small red chilli
¼ teaspoon white pepper
2 tablespoons brown sugar

2 eggplants (aubergines)
vegetable oil, for brushing
lime wedges, to serve

METHOD
Preheat the barbecue grill to high.

To make the sambal, sit the tomatoes, garlic and shallots on the grill and cook for about 8–10 minutes, turning often and removing from the grill when they are charred all over. Wrap the shrimp paste loosely in foil and sit on the grill for 2–3 minutes. When all the ingredients are cool enough to handle, peel the garlic and put the garlic, tomatoes and shallots in a food processor with the shrimp paste, chilli, white pepper and sugar. Process until smooth, then pour into a small saucepan and simmer for about 10 minutes, until slightly thickened. Transfer to a bowl and allow to cool.

To cook the eggplant, preheat the barbecue grill to medium.

Cut each eggplant in half lengthways and make several shallow, diagonal incisions on the flesh side of the eggplant. Brush the cut side with the vegetable oil. Cook, cut side down, on the grill for 8–10 minutes, until golden and charred around the edges. Turn over and cook for another 5 minutes, or until the eggplant has collapsed and is soft.

Serve with the sambal and lime wedges on the side.

MIGAS AND TOMATO SALAD

Serves 4

I'll interpret this in a very broad sense: migas is a dish using leftover bread in Spanish, Portuguese and Mexican cooking. The bread can be soaked in a mixture of milk and water and it is then deep-fried. This is a tasty technique but impossible when cooking outside on a barbecue. Cooking the soaked bread on a hotplate is a convenient alternative, if not a bit healthier.

METHOD

Preheat the barbecue hotplate to high.

Combine the milk and 3 tablespoons of water in a bowl. Soak each slice of bread in this mixture for 1 minute.

Remove the bread from the milk mixture and gently squeeze out as much liquid as possible. Drizzle the hotplate generously with olive oil and cook the bread for a couple of minutes on each side, until golden and crispy around the edges.

Remove the bread and allow to cool. When cool enough to handle, roughly tear the bread and put into a bowl with the tomato, vinegar, garlic and parsley. Season well with salt and freshly ground black pepper, and toss to combine. Serve warm.

INGREDIENTS

3 tablespoons milk
4 slices ciabatta bread
olive oil, for cooking
3 tomatoes, roughly chopped
2 tablespoons red wine vinegar
1 small garlic clove, crushed
1 small handful roughly chopped
    flat-leaf (Italian) parsley

CHARGRILLED FENNEL WITH CHILLI AND HERBS

Serves 4

Fennel in all its forms is delicious. The feathery tops add flavour to dressings and mayonnaise. The beefy bulbs can be cooked in all sorts of ways—in pasta sauces, risotto, minestrone and roasted with pork or chicken. Fennel seeds are a staple in my cupboard, ready to be used in Indian- and Italian-inspired recipes.

INGREDIENTS

4 medium fennel bulbs, preferably
    with tops on
2 garlic cloves, chopped
3 tablespoons olive oil
2 tablespoons red wine vinegar
2 teaspoons dijon mustard
½ teaspoon sea salt
chilli flakes, to taste
1 handful flat-leaf (Italian) parsley,
    finely chopped
1 handful mint, finely chopped

METHOD

If the fennel has feathery tops, cut them off and roughly chop so you have a small handful. Set aside. Slice the fennel lengthways into 0.5 cm (¼ in) thick slices. Put into a bowl with the garlic and 1 tablespoon of the olive oil. Set aside at room temperature for 30 minutes.

Combine the remaining olive oil with the remaining ingredients in a large bowl.

Preheat the barbecue grill to high. Cook half of the fennel slices for 4–5 minutes each side, until golden and charred and the garlic is golden and aromatic. Put the hot fennel in the bowl with the dressing and toss to coat. Repeat with the remaining fennel. Serve warm or at room temperature with the fennel tops sprinkled over.

NAKED SAMOSAS

Serves 4

So called because they have no pastry. This is more like a vegetable patty or burger with all the tasty flavours of Indian cooking. You could serve this up as a take on a veggie burger—put the samosa on a piece of warm, grilled naan bread and top with the chutney, yoghurt and coriander.

METHOD

Peel and wash the potatoes. Cut each into 8 pieces and put into a medium saucepan. Cover with cold water and bring to the boil, cooking for 15 minutes or until just cooked. Drain well then tip the potatoes out onto a clean chopping board to cool and dry.

Put the potatoes into a large bowl and roughly mash.

Heat the olive oil in a frying pan over high heat. Add the mustard seeds and cook until the seeds start to pop. Add the onion and cook, stirring, for about 4–5 minutes, until golden. Add the garlic, ginger, cumin seeds and fennel seeds and stir-fry for 1 minute, until aromatic. Add the peas and mix through. Pour the onion mixture over the potatoes. Add the turmeric, sea salt, chilli powder, garam masala and coriander. Use a large spoon to stir, making sure the ingredients are really well combined. Set aside at room temperature for an hour or two for flavours to develop or refrigerate until needed.

Using slightly wet hands, roughly divide the mixture into 8 equal portions and form into balls. Gently pat down to make a disc or patty.

Preheat the barbecue hotplate to high and drizzle over a little olive oil to grease.

Cook the patties for 10 minutes each side, so they have a golden crust.

Serve with the mango chutney, yoghurt and coriander sprigs.

INGREDIENTS

4 medium russet (idaho) or king edward potatoes
2 tablespoons light olive oil, plus extra, for cooking
½ teaspoon black mustard seeds
1 onion, thinly sliced
1 garlic clove, finely chopped
2 teaspoons finely grated ginger
½ teaspoon cumin seeds
1 teaspoon fennel seeds
75 g (2½ oz/½ cup) frozen peas, defrosted
¼ teaspoon ground turmeric
2 teaspoons sea salt
¼ teaspoon chilli powder
½ teaspoon garam masala
1 small bunch coriander (cilantro), finely chopped
mango chutney, to serve
plain yoghurt, to serve
coriander (cilantro) sprigs, to serve

PANEER AND TOMATO SKEWERS

Serves 6

Paneer is an Indian fresh 'cheese', though not really a cheese in the same sense many of us would think as it doesn't have a setting agent like rennet. Like haloumi, it grills well. It can be cubed or cut into steaks and cooked until golden.

INGREDIENTS

1 large red chilli, thinly sliced on
   an angle
3 tablespoons light olive oil, plus
   extra, for cooking
1 teaspoon sea salt
1 handful roughly chopped
   coriander (cilantro) leaves
1 handful roughly chopped mint
2 tablespoons lemon juice
400 g (14 oz) paneer, cut into
   2–3 cm (¾–1¼ in) cubes
24 cherry tomatoes
1 teaspoon cumin seeds
1 teaspoon fennel seeds
lemon wedges, to serve

METHOD

Combine the chilli, olive oil, sea salt, coriander, mint and lemon juice in a bowl and set aside. Soak 12 bamboo skewers for 30 minutes.

Preheat the barbecue hotplate to high and lightly brush with olive oil to grease.

Thread two pieces of paneer and two tomatoes alternately onto each bamboo skewer. Sprinkle with the cumin and fennel seeds.

Cook the skewers for 8–10 minutes, turning often until the paneer is golden and the tomatoes softened.

Arrange on a serving platter and pour over the dressing. Serve with the lemon wedges.

SPICED PARSNIPS

Serves 4-6

Parsnip is an odd thing to barbecue but I barbecued it in winter, when many of these recipes were tested, and when parsnips are abundant and well priced. This veggie needs to be par-cooked beforehand otherwise it will burn before it is cooked through.

METHOD

Peel the parsnips and cut in half lengthways. Combine the olive oil, turmeric, fennel seeds, cumin seeds, chilli powder and sea salt in a large bowl.

Bring a saucepan of water to the boil. Add the parsnips and cook for 4–5 minutes or until just starting to soften. Drain well and tip the warm parsnips into the bowl with the spiced oil. Toss to coat the parsnips in the spiced oil. Set aside at room temperature for 1 hour.

Preheat the barbecue hotplate to high. Keep the bowl near the barbecue. Lift the parsnips out of the bowl, letting the excess spiced oil drip back into the bowl. Reserve the spiced oil. Cook the parsnips for 5 minutes each side, until tender and slightly charred. Drizzle the spiced oil over the parsnips and cook for just a few more seconds.

Season with the sea salt and freshly ground black pepper to taste. Serve sprinkled with the mint and the lemon wedges on the side.

INGREDIENTS

1 kg (2 lb 4 oz) medium sized
    parsnips
3 tablespoons light olive oil
1 teaspoon ground turmeric
1 teaspoon fennel seeds
1 teaspoon cumin seeds
¼ teaspoon chilli powder
1 teaspoon sea salt
3 tablespoons torn mint leaves
lemon wedges, to serve

THE GARDEN

SICILIAN GRILLED VEGETABLE SALAD

Serves 4–6

I am using eggplant and cauliflower here but you could also use zucchini, broccolini and capsicum. Any veggie will do, really, so long as you add the dressing to the just-cooked vegetables letting them soak up all the tasty bits—kind of like a reverse marinade.

DRESSING
125 ml (4 fl oz/½ cup) olive oil
2 tablespoons red wine vinegar
2 garlic cloves, crushed
1 large handful mint, roughly
    chopped
1 large handful flat-leaf (Italian)
    parsley, roughly chopped
1 handful basil leaves, torn
2 tablespoons small salted capers,
    unrinsed
½ teaspoon sugar
45 g (1¾ oz/¼ cup) raisins

2 medium eggplants (aubergines)
1 small head cauliflower
1 tablespoon light olive oil

METHOD
Combine all the dressing ingredients in a large bowl.
    Preheat the barbecue grill to medium. Slice the eggplant into 1 cm (½ in) rounds and divide the cauliflower into bite-sized florets. Put the vegetables in a bowl with the olive oil and season well with salt and freshly ground black pepper, tossing to coat. Put the eggplant and cauliflower on the grill. Cook for 8–10 minutes. Turn over and cook for another 5 minutes, or until just tender.
    While they are still hot, put the vegetables in a large bowl, pour over the dressing and toss to combine. Cover with plastic wrap and set aside at room temperature for 30 minutes to 1 hour, allowing the flavours to develop. Stir and serve.

POTATOES IN FOIL WITH HERBED LABNEH

Serves 4

Go and get some labneh and try it, please. And use it in all sorts of things as a substitute for all sorts of other things. Put it in dips to replace sour cream. Use it like you would hummus, or yoghurt, which is what it is anyway. You can even use labneh to replace ricotta or cream cheese in sweets like cheesecake.

METHOD

To make the herbed labneh, combine all the ingredients in a bowl and set aside at room temperature, or refrigerate until needed.

Preheat the barbecue hotplate to medium. Wrap each potato in foil. Put on the hotplate, close the lid and cook for 1 hour, turning often, until the potato is tender. You can check if the potato is cooked without unwrapping by pressing down with tongs or a spatula. When cooked the potato will feel soft.

Remove the potatoes and leave wrapped for 10–15 minutes. They can be left on the barbecue lid to keep warm.

Unwrap the potatoes, press down with a spatula to flatten and split the skin and spoon over the herbed labneh while the potatoes are still hot.

HERBED LABNEH

125 g (4½ oz/½ cup) labneh (strained yoghurt)
1 tablespoon finely snipped chives
1 tablespoon finely chopped flat-leaf (Italian) parsley
1 tablespoon finely chopped mint

4 large potatoes, with skin on, washed

SWEET AND SOUR PUMPKIN

Serves 6

Sweet and sour is not a flavour combination unique to Chinese cooking.
The Sicilians are masters too, albeit in a much more subtle way—the combination
of sugar and vinegar is common in southern Italian cooking.

INGREDIENTS
1 small jap or kent (winter squash)
   pumpkin
2 tablespoons rice bran oil

DRESSING
4 tablespoons red wine vinegar
3 tablespoons olive oil
2 garlic cloves, finely chopped
¼ teaspoon chilli flakes
2 teaspoons brown sugar
1 handful mint, coarsely chopped

METHOD
Cut the pumpkin in half using a large knife. Scoop
out the seeds with a large metal spoon and discard.
Lay the cut side of the pumpkin flat on a chopping
board. Use the natural indentations to cut the
pumpkin into thick wedges. Put into a bowl with
the rice bran oil, season well with salt and freshly
ground black pepper and toss to coat the pumpkin
with the oil.

Combine all the dressing ingredients in a bowl
and set aside.

Preheat the barbecue hotplate to medium. Lay
the pumpkin, cut side down, on the hotplate, close
the lid and cook for 10 minutes. Turn the pumpkin
over and cook for another 5–10 minutes, or until
just tender.

Put the hot pumpkin into a large bowl. Pour over
the dressing and toss to combine. Season to taste
with salt and freshly ground black pepper and serve
warm or at room temperature.

SWEET POTATOES IN JACKETS WITH CREAMY FETA

Serves 4

Sweet potato, like potato, cooks up really well on the barbecue: wrapped in foil and cooked until fluffy and soft on the inside with the skin a little chewy and sweet. I like the notion of being able to do a couple of things and do them really well. A mate of mine does a sweet potato and grilled chicken dish. He cooks both to perfection without any flavouring. Now that's stripping back to bare barbecue basics!

FETA AND DILL CREAM

100 g (3½ oz) soft feta
    cheese, crumbled
1 garlic clove, crushed
3 tablespoons chopped dill
2 tablespoons olive oil
2 tablespoons milk

1 large sweet potato, peeled
4 tablespoons olive oil
1 teaspoon sea salt

METHOD

To make the feta and dill cream, put the feta cheese, garlic, dill and olive oil in a food processor and process to a thick paste. With the motor running, add the milk, processing until thick and creamy. Set aside.

Cut the pointy ends off the sweet potato and cut into four portions, roughly equal in size.

Preheat the barbecue hotplate to medium.

Tear off four sheets of foil, large enough to wrap each piece of sweet potato entirely. Sit a piece of sweet potato in the centre of each piece of foil. Pour 1 tablespoon of olive oil on each and sprinkle with the sea salt. Loosely wrap in the foil and sit on the hotplate. Close the lid and cook for 45 minutes, or until the sweet potato is very tender.

Unwrap the sweet potato and spoon the feta and dill cream over while still hot.

AROMATIC TOFU AND MUSHROOM SKEWERS

Serves 3

Okay, so I like both meat and tofu. Is that a crime? Choose your tofu wisely. Avoid any silken or soft tofu. These will just not work on the barbecue. This is dark, aromatic and exotic.

METHOD

If the tofu is not already portioned, cut it into 12 equal-sized shapes.

Put the soy sauce, sugar, star anise, cinnamon stick and whole cloves in a saucepan and bring to the boil, stirring to dissolve the sugar. While still warm, pour the soy mixture over the tofu and set aside at room temperature for 3 hours, turning the tofu pieces every 30 minutes.

Preheat the barbecue hotplate to high.

Thread 2 pieces of tofu, one of each of the mushrooms and two pieces of spring onion onto each of six metal skewers.

Brush the hotplate with vegetable oil. Cook the skewers for 5 minutes. Use a spatula to turn them over, being careful not to break the tofu. Cook for another 5 minutes, until the tofu is dark and the mushrooms are tender.

INGREDIENTS

820 g (1 lb 13 oz) medium firm tofu
250 ml (9 fl oz/1 cup) light soy sauce
1 teaspoon sugar
2 star anise
1 cinnamon stick
2 whole cloves
6 shiitake mushrooms
6 Swiss brown mushrooms
2 spring onions (scallions), cut into
    12 x 3–4 cm (1¼–1½ in) lengths
vegetable oil, for cooking

CHARGRILLED WITLOF WITH PARSLEY, LEMON AND PECORINO

This recipe may well epitomise many of the great things about barbecuing, even though no meat is involved, as well as many of the great things we associate with rustic, Italian cooking. Take a raw ingredient. Don't mess with it too much—just grill until golden, sweet and slightly charred and serve with some herbs, lemon juice and cheese. Nice.

METHOD

Preheat the barbecue hotplate to medium–high and lightly brush with the olive oil to grease. Put the witlof, cut side up, on the hotplate and cook for 5 minutes, or until golden. Turn over and cook for another 5 minutes, or until tender. Put the hot witlof in a large bowl with the sea salt, freshly ground black pepper, parsley, lemon juice and pecorino cheese. Toss to combine and serve warm.

INGREDIENTS

light olive oil, for cooking
8 witlof (chicory/Belgian endive),
    cut in half lengthways
1 teaspoon sea salt
1 handful roughly chopped
    flat-leaf (Italian) parsley
2 tablespoons lemon juice
2 tablespoons finely grated
    pecorino cheese

SOY AND GINGER GRILLED MUSHROOMS

Serves 4

Try not to use really tiny mushrooms here or for any barbecue cooking for that matter. Little ones are a pain to cook. Big, steaky mushies are easy to cook, have more flesh and are tastier.

INGREDIENTS
250 ml (9 fl oz/1 cup) red wine
250 ml (9 fl oz/1 cup) light soy sauce
2 tablespoons rice flour
1 tablespoon sesame oil
1 tablespoon finely grated ginger
6 king oyster mushrooms, halved
    lengthways
6 large shiitake mushrooms
6 large Swiss brown mushrooms
2 tablespoons rice bran oil
100 g (3½ oz) oyster mushrooms
sliced spring onions (scallions),
    to serve

METHOD
Combine the red wine, soy sauce, rice flour, sesame oil and ginger in a large bowl. Add the mushrooms, except the oyster mushrooms, tossing to coat in the marinade and set aside at room temperature for 3 hours, or cover and refrigerate for 6 hours.

Preheat the barbecue hotplate to high. Pour the rice bran oil over the hotplate to grease.

Remove the mushrooms from the marinade and tumble onto the hotplate. Cook for 10–15 minutes, turning the mushrooms often until dark, tender and aromatic. Add the small oyster mushrooms and cook, turning, for 1–2 minutes or until just tender. Serve hot, with the spring onions scattered over.

SILVERBEET AND FETA GÖZLEME

Serves 4

Hot dog and donut stalls have been replaced by gözleme (Turkish pizza) stalls at markets. And this is not a bad thing. I love these 'pizzas'. It would be very tricky to try your hand at making the dough yourself but you don't have to, not with so many exotic pre-made breads out there, including some good gluten-free ones too.

METHOD

Combine the olive oil, onion, garlic, silverbeet, cheeses and paprika in a bowl, mixing well to combine.

Spread half of the mixture over one pitta bread and top with another. Repeat with the remaining pitta breads and filling to make a second gözleme.

Preheat the barbecue hotplate to medium–high. Brush both sides of the gözleme with oil. Cook the gözleme one at a time for 3–4 minutes each side, using a spatula to compress it, until crisp and golden. Cut into wedges and serve with lots of fresh lemon juice squeezed over. Cook the second gözleme while your guests eat the first.

INGREDIENTS

1 tablespoon olive oil, plus extra, for cooking
1 red onion, finely chopped
2 garlic cloves, crushed
180 g (6 oz) finely shredded silverbeet (Swiss chard)
200 g (7 oz) feta cheese, crumbled
50 g (1¾ oz/½ cup) coarsely grated cheddar cheese
¼ teaspoon sweet paprika
4 x 26 cm (10½ in) Greek pitta breads
lemons wedges, to serve

BARBIE GHANOUSH

Serves 4–8

This one is made for the barbecue. Actually, I don't believe you can achieve the same flavour result without cooking eggplant over a naked flame. The smokiness of the charred skin somehow gets into the flesh of the eggplant with really very little cooking time.

INGREDIENTS

2 large eggplants (aubergines)
2 teaspoons sea salt
3 tablespoons lemon juice
3 garlic cloves, crushed
2 tablespoons extra virgin olive oil,
    plus extra, to serve
chargrilled Lebanese bread, to
    serve

METHOD

Preheat the barbecue grill to high.

Prick the eggplants several times with a fork. Cook the eggplants on the barbecue for 10–15 minutes, turning often, until collapsed and tender. Remove and allow to cool on a tray.

When cool enough to handle, strip off the eggplants' skins and discard. Place the flesh in a sieve over a bowl and set aside for 15 minutes to drain. Put the eggplant flesh in a food processor with the sea salt, lemon juice, garlic and olive oil and process to a purée. Pour the spread into a bowl, drizzle with the extra olive oil and serve with the chargrilled bread.

MUSHROOMS STUFFED WITH MANCHEGO RAREBIT

Serves 4

Manchego is a Spanish cheese, not unlike cheddar. This is a hybrid of a fondue and Welsh rarebit. Again, like in other mushie recipes, feel free to substitute those listed for other varieties, so long as they are not petit.

METHOD

To make the manchego rarebit, combine the beer and cheese in a small saucepan. Cook over medium heat, stirring until the mixture is smooth.

Preheat the barbecue hotplate to medium. Sit the saucepan on a warm part of the barbecue to keep the mixture gooey.

Put a sheet of baking paper on the hotplate and lightly brush with olive oil to grease. Cook the mushrooms, cap side down, for 8–10 minutes, or until tender. Turn over and spoon the rarebit into the caps. Close the lid and cook for 5 minutes, until the cheese has melted and the mushrooms are tender.

Sprinkle over the paprika and the parsley to serve.

INGREDIENTS

125 ml (4 fl oz/½ cup) beer
200 g (7 oz/2 cups) grated
    manchego cheese
olive oil, for cooking
12 medium field mushrooms
smoked paprika, to serve
flat-leaf (Italian) parsley sprigs, to
    serve

RED CABBAGE AND BACON SALAD

Serves 4–6

Warm salads will be really enjoyed by your barbecue guests. Spinach leaves and witlof can substitute for the cabbage, served up with pork chops, chicken or lamb.

DRESSING
2 garlic cloves, crushed
3 tablespoons olive oil
2 tablespoons red wine vinegar
2 tablespoons chopped tarragon
2 tablespoons roughly chopped
    flat-leaf (Italian) parsley

1 small red cabbage
olive oil, for cooking
6 bacon slices, rind removed

METHOD
Combine all the dressing ingredients in a bowl and set aside.

Preheat the barbecue grill and hotplate to high.

Pull away any tough leaves from the cabbage. Trim most of the stem off, leaving just enough to help the cabbage hold together when cooked. Cut 1 cm (½ in) wide strips from top to stem of the cabbage.

Drizzle the hotplate with olive oil. Lay the cabbage on the hotplate and sprinkle with sea salt. Lay the bacon on the grill.

Cook the cabbage and bacon for 4–5 minutes each side, until the cabbage is golden and the bacon is starting to crisp up. Turn both cabbage and bacon over and cook for another 2–3 minutes.

Put the cabbage in a large bowl and while still hot add the dressing. Roughly chop the bacon and add to the salad. Toss to combine and serve warm.

INDEX

ACKNOWLEDGEMENTS

It really is such a total joy to work with the Murdoch Books team. Thanks to all those involved in producing this book.

I also want to give a special thanks to Kay Scarlett and Juliet Rogers. Thanks, gals, for your support over the years.

I am pretty fortunate to have a crack at a follow up to *Fired Up*. This doesn't happen too often in the world of food publishing. Thanks to all those fans of *Fired Up*. Without you this book would never have happened.

Roscoe

First published in 2012 by Murdoch Books Pty Ltd

Murdoch Books Australia
Pier 8/9, 23 Hickson Road
Millers Point NSW 2000
Phone: +61 (0) 2 8220 2000
Fax: +61 (0) 2 8220 2558
www.murdochbooks.com.au
info@murdochbooks.com.au

Murdoch Books UK
Erico House, 6th Floor
93–99 Upper Richmond Road
Putney, London SW15 2TG
Phone: +44 (0) 20 8785 5995
www.murdochbooks.co.uk
info@murdochbooks.co.uk

For Corporate Orders & Custom Publishing contact Noel Hammond,
National Business Development Manager Murdoch Books Australia

Publisher: Sally Webb
Designer: Hugh Ford
Photographer: Nicky Ryan
Stylist: Sarah O'Brien
Editor: Paul O'Beirne
Food Editor: Michelle Earl
Project Manager: Claire Grady
Production Controller: Joan Beal

National Library of Australia
Author: Dobson, Ross, 1965-
Title: More fired up : no nonsense barbecuing / Ross Dobson.
ISBN: 9781742664316 (hbk)
Notes: Includes index.
Subjects: Barbecuing.
Dewey Number: 641.5784

Printed by 1010 Printing, China

IMPORTANT: Those who might be at risk from the effects of salmonella poisoning (the elderly,
pregnant women, young children and those suffering from immune deficiency diseases) should
consult their doctor with any concerns about eating raw eggs.

CONVERSION GUIDE: Cooking times may vary depending on the oven you are using. For fan-
forced ovens, as a general rule, set the oven temperature to 20°C (35°F) lower than indicated
in the recipe. We have used 20 ml (4 teaspoon) tablespoon measures. If you are using a 15 ml
(3 teaspoon) tablespoon, add an extra teaspoon for each tablespoon specified.